The Literary Agenda

Tradition

The Literary Agenda

Tradition

A Feeling for the Literary Past

SETH LERER

OXFORD
UNIVERSITY PRESS

OXFORD
UNIVERSITY PRESS

Great Clarendon Street, Oxford, OX2 6DP,
United Kingdom

Oxford University Press is a department of the University of Oxford.
It furthers the University's objective of excellence in research, scholarship,
and education by publishing worldwide. Oxford is a registered trade mark of
Oxford University Press in the UK and in certain other countries

First Edition published in 2016

Impression: 1

Published in the United States of America by Oxford University Press
198 Madison Avenue, New York, NY 10016, United States of America

British Library Cataloguing in Publication Data
Data available

Library of Congress Control Number: 2016934698

ISBN 978–0–19–873628–8

Printed in Great Britain by
Clays Ltd, St Ives plc

Series Introduction

The Crisis in, the Threat to, the Plight of the Humanities: enter these phrases in Google's search engine and there are 23 million results, in a great fifty-year-long cry of distress, outrage, fear, and melancholy. Grant, even, that every single anxiety and complaint in that catalogue of woe is fully justified—the lack of public support for the arts, the cutbacks in government funding for the humanities, the imminent transformation of a literary and verbal culture by visual/virtual/digital media, the decline of reading... And still, though it were all true, and just because it might be, there would remain the problem of the response itself. Too often there's recourse to the shrill moan of offended piety or a defeatist withdrawal into professionalism.

The Literary Agenda is a series of short polemical monographs that believes there is a great deal that needs to be said about the state of literary education inside schools and universities and more fundamentally about the importance of literature and of reading in the wider world. The category of "the literary" has always been contentious. What *is* clear, however, is how increasingly it is dismissed or is unrecognized as a way of thinking or an arena for thought. It is skeptically challenged from within, for example, by the sometimes rival claims of cultural history, contextualized explanation, or media studies. It is shaken from without by even greater pressures: by economic exigency and the severe social attitudes that can follow from it; by technological change that may leave the traditional forms of serious human communication looking merely antiquated. For just these reasons this is the right time for renewal, to start reinvigorated work into the meaning and value of literary reading for the sake of the future.

It is certainly no time to retreat within institutional walls. For all the academic resistance to "instrumentalism," to governmental measurements of public impact and practical utility, literature exists in and across society. The "literary" is not pure or specialized or self-confined; it is not restricted to the practitioner in writing or the academic in studying. It exists in the whole range of the world which is its subject-matter: it consists in what non-writers actively receive from writings when, for example, they start to see the world more imaginatively as a result of reading novels and begin to think more carefully about human personality. It comes from literature making available much of human life that would not otherwise be existent to thought or recognizable as knowledge. If it is true that involvement in literature, so far from being a minority aesthetic, represents a significant contribution to the life of human thought, then that idea has to be argued at the public level without succumbing to a hollow rhetoric or bowing to a reductive worldview. Hence the effort of this series to take its place *between* literature and the world. The double-sided commitment to occupying that place and establishing its reality is the only "agenda" here, without further prescription as to what should then be thought or done within it.

What is at stake is not simply some defensive or apologetic "justification" in the abstract. The case as to why literature matters in the world not only has to be argued conceptually and strongly tested by thought, it should be given presence, performed, and brought to life in the way that literature itself does. That is why this series includes the writers themselves, the novelists and poets, in order to try to close the gap between the thinking of the artists and the thinking of those who read and study them. It is why it also involves other kinds of thinkers—the philosopher, the theologian, the psychologist, the neuroscientist—examining the role of literature within their own life's work and thought, and the effect of that work, in turn, upon literary thinking. This series admits and encourages personal voices in an unpredictable variety of individual approach and expression, speaking wherever possible across countries and disciplines and temperaments. It aims for something more than intellectual assent: rather the literary sense of what it is like to feel the thought, to embody an idea in a person, to bring it to being in a narrative or in aid of adventurous reflection. If the artists refer to their own works, if other thinkers return to ideas that have marked much of their working life, that is not their vanity nor a failure of originality. It is what the series has asked of them: to speak out of what they know and care about, in whatever language can best serve their most serious thinking, and without the necessity of trying to cover every issue or meet every objection in each volume.

Philip Davis

Preface: "Today, makes Yesterday mean"

This is a book about tradition in the literary imagination. It asks how we can have an unironic, affective relationship to the literary past in an age marked by historical self-consciousness, critical distance, and shifts in cultural literacy. It ranges through a set of fiction, poetry, and criticism that makes up our inherited traditions and that also confronts the question of a literary canon and its personal and historical meaning. How are we taught to have a felt experience of literary objects? How do we make our personal anthologies of reading to shape social selves? Why should we care about what literature does both to and for us?

As a contribution to The Literary Agenda, my book speaks to the provocations of this series' editor. Philip Davis, in his introduction to his *Reading and the Reader*, affirms that "the category of the 'literary' has always been contentious," and that we need to broaden our discussions to embrace the reader both inside and outside the classroom. The act of reading, Davis claims, "is something that must be done...inside specific examples." I organize this book, therefore, around the ways in which particular works of literature address the nature of the literary tradition, its social value, and its personal impact. Davis affirms that, in a life of reading, we may walk away from certain books, only to have them come back, later on, with new importance or effect. My writers here were all great readers. Dickens and Orwell, Rushdie and Bradbury, Dickinson and Frost, Anne Bradstreet and Gjertrud Schnackenberg, Chaucer, Dante, Virgil—all built their literary structures on the scaffold of their bookshelves. I am concerned, then, not only with what Davis calls the ways in which "the fictional becomes real." I am concerned with how the lines between the real and fictional are always blurry.[1]

Books in this series aspire to be "short polemical monographs." Here is mine: this book affirms the value of close and nuanced reading for our understanding of both past and present. Tradition, in my view, is not a thing, it is an activity. To work within tradition is to make anew, not just to curate. Mine is a book of feelings and convictions, but it is also book of scholarship. I am, by sensibility and schooling, a historian of literature and a close reader of texts, delighting in the play of language. I get great pleasure from discovering a source or recognizing a repeated motif or finding images and structures. I marvel at a writer's skill. I revel in my own research abilities.

But I am, too, a product of my academic generation. Since coming out of college in the 1970s, I have observed and participated in the rise of a linguistically oriented literary theory, in the challenges posed by cultural critiques of race and class and gender, and in the increasing estrangement of academic literature professors from the common readers of a public that, to some extent, believes we do not love or learn from books. I do not advocate a return to a time of affective appreciation. I do not wish to efface forty years of theoretical and critical professionalization. I do not think that literature—on its own, untainted by teachers or unmarked by critics—offers a univocal set of authorial intentions which, once discovered, ends any process of interpretation.

And yet, I feel. I became a professor because I enjoyed the act of reading and interpreting. I believe that the job of criticism should be the productive display of creative understanding: an ongoing attempt to make sense of texts that are distant from ourselves. I also believe that we need continually to reread those texts. To read a book at twenty is to have a different experience than reading that same book at fifty. *David Copperfield* means something different to a college freshman than to a parent. *1984* or *Fahrenheit 451* are more than science-fiction entertainments to a former university bureaucrat. Frost's "After Apple-Picking" becomes more than a nature poem when you read it with the mind of an allegorist. There are so many different ways to read, and in a lifetime we may try out several of them. "One cannot read a book," said Vladimir Nabokov. "One can only reread it."[2] Every encounter with a book changes that book and us; when we come to that book once again, we have been changed by living and by literature.

To read the tradition is always to read it in the now. We try to reconstruct historical environments; we seek to hear as others heard. But, as Emily Dickinson put it, "Today, makes Yesterday mean."[3] That is my sense of the tradition: a continuous process in which we see the past through the present. But more than that, it is the present that gives meaning to the past. It is our hindsight that discerns the patterns from which we make meaning out of disparate experiences. And in making meaning out of yesterday, we find purpose in today.

My purpose here is to explore the ways in which the literary past makes us. This is no history of great works, nor is it a review of forms and genres, authors, and periods. This is a study of how literary and critical works generate and respond to traditions of reading and writing. My field is writing in the English language, but what I do may speak to recent reassessments of the literary past in other languages and cultures. Marc Fumaroli, for example, has illuminated how the French discovery of classical rhetoric in the seventeenth century generated a tradition of European discourse in which culture served diplomacy, governance expressed a style, and "modernity" itself grew out of a negotiation between past and present.[4] The German scholar Harald Weinrich, too, has sought to understand how literary traditions shape social worlds—but in his work, it has been less a matter of remembering and revering the past than creatively forgetting it. Weinrich has imagined a cultural tradition of forgetting, a habit of mind that effaces the past only to recreate it, a tradition of reading keyed to loss as much as to recovery.[5] These scholars, and a host of others working in world literatures, have taught me that "tradition" does not simply mean the past. Nor does it singularly imply conservatism, preservation, or unthinking reverence. Tradition lies at the intersection of the history of literature and the literary canon. It sits across the past and the present.

For, on the one hand, literature has a history. Writers follow each other, and literary works have value and meaning in the times and places that created and received them. They have value, too, in subsequent times and places, and the story of literature is precisely that, a story. We have created narratives of forms and genres, writers and periods, to give a framework for our understanding. A phrase such as "the rise of the novel" implies, by necessity, a linear trajectory. A phrase such as "epic and empire" implies, by equal need, a temporal relationship between a literary form and a political entity. A phrase such as "nation and narration" similarly implies that literary stories create and maintain identities of language, land, and power. All these phrases (themselves titles of defining critical works of the last sixty years) make literature into a historically grounded tale, with individual works located like pinpoints on an arc of development.[6]

But, on the other hand, the canon does not work like that. Canons are fixed things. They exist not in a historical narrative but in a moment. A list of great books, or of best poems, or favorite novels, plays, or writers, is precisely that, a list. It exists in the simultaneity of the syllabus, the bookshelf, or the backpack. Canons are collections of texts for a particular time or person or event. If literary history is horizontal, canons are vertical. A literary tradition, thus, is the assembly of works and writers, drawn from history, but realigned into an object of study or pleasure or teaching.

Much of what I have to say, I hope, will speak to teachers and students of world literary traditions. No Anglo-American reader, any more, can content him- or herself with English alone. We live among languages. On my California campus I can go a full day listening to speech that I can recognize but not reproduce. Spanish, Mandarin, Korean, Amharic, Russian, Hindi, and Farsi sing across the quads. On a recent sabbatical at Oxford, I heard animated conversations in Arabic, Urdu, Dutch, and German in the Bodleian Library tea room. My attentions to the tradition in English, therefore, are not designed to exclude the rest of the globe. A fair amount of what I have to say concerns writers who have explicitly reflected on their émigré or newly arrived status in a new world: Salman Rushdie, Anne Bradstreet, Leo Spitzer. Orwell, for all his mastery of English, read Dante in Italian. Robert Frost wrote his New England poems while living in Great Britain. Some of the most beautiful and poignant poetry in American English has been written by a poet named Gjertrud Schnackenberg. And while I return, in my final chapter, to the most traditional of core authors in the Western tradition—Homer, Virgil, Chaucer, and Milton—I do so through the lens of digitalized literacy. Teaching in a world of Facebook and the Internet raises questions about how immediate the literary experience can be and what happens when we create simulacra of our selves for others not to see but read.

The Anglo-American literary tradition has always been a world tradition, engaged with the languages and cultures of non-English speaking peoples and attentive to changes in the media of literacy. But what I believe to be distinctive about this tradition is the way in which it has self-consciously seen itself *as* a tradition: the way in which its writers and critics have concerned themselves with the relationship of past to present; the way in which the very word "tradition" has taken on a powerful, cultural meaning, very different from how the word and its cognates work in other languages.[7]

I have fifty thousand words to work with. I must be selective. Each chapter of my book explores how writers adjudicate between the historical and the canonical, between the linearity of influence and the moment of evaluation. I have chosen writers that are familiar to me and, I imagine, familiar to most readers. But I have chosen writers, too, who skew tradition and, in the process, assure their places in anthologies or syllabi, the website and the blog, the public and the school library. Some of the critics I discuss are monumental (Eliot), controversial (Said), newly revived (Trilling), out-of-date (Leavis), known only to specialists (Spitzer), or not even thought of as literary critics at all (Benjamin Spock). Some of them are my contemporaries (Franco Moretti, Judith Butler); some will outlive me (Denise Gigante, Leah Price, Deirdre Lynch, Jeff Nunokawa). This is a book that does not prompt the reader to ask: what about *my* favorites? It is a book that prompts you to ask: how does it change the way I read my favorites?

I hope these readings and responses can provide a template for your own engagement with a text and with your own attempts to locate yourself along lines of influence and inspiration. But I hope, too, that you will find an argument for why and how the academic study of the literary past can both invigorate and challenge you: as a student, a teacher, a reader, or a writer. Hayden White, one of the most original and influential literary critics of the last forty years, has long argued for the ways in which all forms of narrative draw on figures of rhetoric and turns of metaphor. The linear accounts of history, he has claimed, take on literary form because their facts are often couched in figurative language, twists of phrasing, similes, and symbols.[8] His work has illustrated how history lives in language, and most recently he has argued for the importance of recognizing how our lives in language place us back in history. White puts the case for the historical interpretation of literature in the modern university with force and eloquence:

> We are interested in placing a writer in his or her context, assessing the extent to which he or she illuminates a time and place and situation, provides insight into the human condition, and so on.... It is true that academic scholars will always tend to

historicize any writer's work. And to historicize is, inevitably, to ironize, of which no one wishes to be the object. Academic critics need "theory" in a way that the writer-as-critic does not. This is because the academic scholar cannot trade on his or her "feelings" as a substitute for analysis of a text. Writers may not like being subjected to analysis rather than met with awe and reverence, but theoretically motivated response to literary or even poetic works represents a kind of criticism that is just as "serious" as any [other kind of] response.[9]

White's points are worth developing. The scholar/critic sees all works of literature as gaining meaning, at least in part, from the moment of their making and reception. As readers, we too are placed in a specific social and historical moment. The job of the critic is to adjudicate, productively, between these two "historicized" experiences. To be placed in history is to be removed from immediacies of feeling and made subject to conditions we may not control. Nobody, White notes, really likes to be taken as a product of history; nobody likes to be analyzed as an object. Those of us who are writers may wish to be met with awe and reverence—or at the very least, to be liked, or enjoyed, or respected. And yet, the academic scholar analyzes.

We may feel awe or reverence to the literary past. That does not prevent us from analyzing it. But, in that scholarly analysis, I do not lose my feelings for a work. My feelings are enhanced. To chart the ways a writer has manipulated, quoted, or alluded to past works shows me that writer's knowledge and sensibility. The simple fact is I enjoy it all.

That is what I wish to convey here: that feeling and analysis are reinforcing; that the literary past can be the subject of inquiry and the object of reverence; that the historical and critical engagement with tradition provides insight into the human condition. Today makes yesterday mean.

Notes

1. Philip Davis, *Reading and the Reader* (Oxford: Oxford University Press, 2013), these quotations from vii, ix, 121, 101. See, too, Davis, *The Experience of Reading* (London: Routledge, 1992).

2. Vladimir Nabokov, *Lectures on Literature*, ed. Fredson Bowers (New York: Harcourt Brace Jovanovich, 1980), 3. Nabokov expands on his paradox: "A good reader, a

major reader, an active and creative reader is a rereader…When we read a book for the first time the very process of laboriously moving our eyes from left to right, line after line, page after page, this complicated physical work upon the book, this stands between us and artistic appreciation."

3. Emily Dickinson to Thomas W. Higginson, July 1862, in Emily Dickinson, Thomas Herbert Johnson, and Theodora Ward, *The Letters of Emily Dickinson* (Cambridge: Mass., Harvard University Press, 1986), 412.

4. Marc Fumaroli, *When the World Spoke French*, trans. Richard Howard (New York: New York Review Books, 2010), and *La République des lettres* (Paris: Gallimard, 2014).

5. Harald Weinrich, *Lethe: Kunst und Kritik des Vergessens* (Munich: C. H. Beck, 1997), trans. Steven Rendall, *Lethe: The Art and Critique of Forgetting* (Ithaca: Cornell University Press, 2004). "For moderns, recollection, which now splits off from the general European memory-tradition, is a privatized kind of memory that has been cut down to its own experiential dimensions. Recollections are therefore in principle always 'my' recollections" (trans. Rendall, 136).

6. Ian Watt, *The Rise of the Novel* (London: Chatto & Windus, 1957); David Quint, *Epic and Empire* (Princeton: Princeton University Press, 1993); Homi Bhabha, *Nation and Narration* (London: Routledge, 1990).

7. See Edward Said, *Culture and Imperialism* (New York: Knopf, 1993), e.g., "British, French, and American imperial experience…has a unique coherence and a special cultural centrality," and furthermore, that because "narrative plays such a remarkable part in the imperial quest, it is therefore not surprising that France and (especially England) have an unbroken tradition of novel-writing, unparalleled elsewhere" (xxii).

8. See *Metahistory: The Historical Imagination in Nineteenth-Century Europe* (Baltimore: Johns Hopkins University Press, 1975) and the essay "The Value of Narrativity in the Representation of Reality," *Critical Inquiry* 7 (1980): 5–27.

9. I quote from White's Facebook post, originally posted May 5, 2015.

Contents

1

Traditions of Tradition

"In recent years the study of literature in our universities has again and again been called into question, chiefly on the ground that what is being studied is not so much literature itself as the history of literature." Lionel Trilling's opening provocation in his essay, "The Sense of the Past," first published in the *Partisan Review* in 1942, could still stand today as an epigraph for any book addressed to academics and lay readers.[1] Take his word "history" and replace it with "theory," or "politics," or "culture," or "socio-economics," or any one of a range of mediating terms and you have the dilemma of the literary classroom. More acutely now than in Trilling's time, literary study, and the humanities in general, have questioned whether there is an autonomous, aesthetic object for its study. At stake is not simply whether we have abandoned appreciation for analysis, or personal response for theoretical meditation. At stake is literature's status as a fulcrum between past and present. Is a writer's meaning, we may ask, a fixed and stable thing, pulled from the past, or is it something ever changing, made and remade by a history of readers? Indeed, are there "writers" and "readers" at all, or only acts of writing and reading?[2]

These questions have been asked since Antiquity. Scholiasts, commentators, pedagogues, critics, journalists, philologists, professors—pick a marker of authority and judgment and you confront the idea of *tradition*. The word comes from the Latin, *traditio*, meaning a handing down, a surrendering, and a delivery from one group to another. *The Oxford English Dictionary* (*OED*)—that most authoritative bearer of linguistic tradition—ranks its definitions of "tradition" and its illustrative quotations historically. Thus, one comes to its entry to find "handing over," "a giving up, surrender, betrayal," and "the surrender of sacred books during time of persecution." Only in the third section of its definitions do we find something akin to what we think tradition is: the

oral delivery of teaching or law, and then long afterwards, "an embod-
iment of old established custom or institution" (def. 5).[3]

Whatever we may think tradition means, or however we may feel
about its acceptance or rejection, this foray into the lexicography
reveals much. It shows that behind the word and its own history there
lies a sense of power and control, of passing on but also giving up. Is
our adherence to tradition, one might ask in this lexicographical
spirit, a ceding of authority? Is it a sacrifice of self, of our originality
to something old, established, customary, and institutional? Or is it,
instead, our participation in a rich and valued set of practices, a way
of cultivating belonging? Tradition is, and always has been, about
knowledge and power, about the individual's relation to the group.
The study of the literary tradition becomes essential to defining what
we do as scholars and teachers. But it remains essential, too, for anyone
who finds (or loses) him- or herself in a book.

The notion of a literary tradition seems quite recent. An advanced
search of the terms in the online *OED* offers the earliest quotation
from Edmund Gosse in 1912: "they were all engaged in keeping
bright, and handing on unquenched, the torch of literary tradition."[4]
Whether or not the phrase was current before Gosse, the idea clearly
was: in Matthew Arnold's notion of the "touchstone" of poetic value;
in Walter Pater's sense of the aesthetic legacy of the past; in John
Ruskin's understanding of the sublime as an artistically mediated
experience of nature, shaped through an appreciation of the place of
styles in history. Our notion of a literary tradition in this specific, cul-
turally validating sense is largely a Victorian construction. True, there
were canons of texts and writers throughout Western literate history,
and true, it had long been the purpose of the scholar and the saint to
pass on valued lessons from that textualized past. But it does seem
clear that only with the nineteenth century's sense of a distinctive,
vernacular body of literature keyed to the maintenance of cultural
authority does our intuitive feeling for a literary tradition fully crystal-
lize. The nineteenth-century imagination of the past, of history itself,
gave rise to new ideas of period and canon, and it lies in this new sense
of history that "literary history" emerges as a category of thought.[5]

An act of surrender or a light of culture, an imposition of authority
or an illumination of the past? Part of what Trilling and his contemporaries, English and American, were writing against was the legacy

of this Victorian critical sensibility. The critics of his generation marked their territory with the spoor of Freud and Marx, with an awareness of how Modernism fragmented the built worlds of experience and memory, and with a new sense of the experimental possibilities of prose and verse. The politics of literature had changed, and the old ideals of "national virtues," as Trilling put it in his essay on Kipling, had changed. "In our day, the idea of the nation has become doubtful and debilitated all over the world."[6] Little wonder that Trilling and his contemporaries had anxieties about tradition in an age of literary innovation and political upheaval. "But even in our own culture with its ambivalent feeling about tradition, there inheres in a work of art of the past a certain quality, an element of its aesthetic existence, which we can identify as its pastness."[7]

It is not difficult for us to see comparable ambivalences now. National identity in all forms remains, if not doubtful, then at least under debate. The place of literature in politics has changed. Louis Menand has put it, "cultural taste has largely been liberated from politics...Art and literature are understood to be too polysemous to sustain a politics. This has given criticism less moral and political work to do."[8] And yet, criticism still has immense cultural and social work to do. Digital media and social networks have, in the first decades of the twenty-first century, redefined relationships of literacy to individual identity. Higher education has become instrumentalized: no longer, many lament, do young people go to university or college to be broadened or cultured; they go to be explicitly prepared for a social and financial success. And our cultural ideals no longer center on the acquisition of knowledge but on the control of data. The central dogma of the information age, perhaps, was expressed by Claude Shannon—the pioneer of information theory who, in the 1940s developed what he called "a mathematical theory of cryptography." Shannon's maxim, "meaning is irrelevant," declared that information could be handled with a greater freedom if it were treated as an abstraction independent of meaning.[9]

My book argues for the personal, felt life in literary history. It argues that an understanding of the literary past remains inseparable from an engagement with the society and the materials that transmit that past and with the institutional practices of criticism and teaching that have mediated it. The study of tradition in its broadest senses goes beyond a claim on the past. It offers up a claim on the present, on the experience of character, of language, of narrative, and of the object that we hold in our hands. Whether that object is a printed page or pixeled screen, it is an object, and we establish a relationship to it that grants us access to imagination.

And when we come upon that object, we invariably ask, why? Our relationship to literature often becomes a questioning of its utility. When we read, we often ask ourselves why are we reading: for entertainment, for instruction, to participate in a long conversation with the past or to escape our present in a world of the imagination? We understand that literature *has* value, but our acts of reading constantly query that sense of value. These meditations and reflections do not undermine the value of literature. They texture it. They make each reading something new and strange. And in our current age of irony and parody, tweets and texts, these meditations are all the more important. They help us find a place for literary experience in a world increasingly suspicious of sincerity.

I begin here by reviewing the traditions of tradition—by looking at the ways in which the term has been invoked (for good and bad) by a variety of literary critics. I then seek to expose the set of concepts that lie behind the idea of literary tradition: concepts such as canon, imitation, representation, and taste. The story of these ideas contributes to a broader understanding of both how and why we have, still, an "ambivalent feeling about tradition." This story helps us understand just why tradition is something that we should "feel" anything about, and what the broader relationship is between the pursuit of knowledge and the cultivation of sensibility in the histories of reading, writing, and teaching. The critics I explore—and, one could argue, every critic from Antiquity to the present—questioned the nature of the literary work: to see it either (to return to Trilling's phrasing) "as the agent of power" or "as the object of knowledge." That, to me, is the fundamental question about literature and society, and this book hopes to provoke new interventions into our debates and our discriminations.

Any discussion of the literary tradition must begin with T. S. Eliot. A century ago, he all but made the word his own in his essay, "Tradition and the Individual Talent" (1917).[10] There, Eliot proposed that the "tradition" was more than the sum of things inherited. It was something to be worked for, gained, and used through the development of a "historical sense," and "a perception, not only of the pastness of the past, but of its presence."[11] Such personalized historicism led, in Eliot's polemic, to the poet's necessary "escape from emotion." His argument sought to divert the reader's attention away from the writer and to the written artifact, and he opened the way (along with such twentieth-century critics as I. A. Richards, John Crowe Ransom, Cleanth Brooks, and Austin Warren) to the New Critical formalism that dominated the Anglo-American classroom for half a century. The principles of "close reading" that developed in this critical tradition hinged not only on a conviction that a work of literature—poem, play, or novel—offered all the information that a reader needed. It hinged, as well, on a conviction that the practice of studying and teaching the work of literature needed little else but literary text and reader's mind. Forms of reading had become inseparable from forms of teaching, and the classroom was the place of preservation: the shared site in which the student and the teacher found the presence of the past.[12]

Eliot sought to establish an ordered understanding of the history of literary reason in the last throes of the Great War. Avowing that the writer must develop a "consciousness of the past" and develop such a consciousness "throughout his career," he remarked: "What happens is a continual surrender of himself as he is at the moment to something which is more valuable. The progress of an artist is a continual self-sacrifice, a continual extinction of personality."[13] The language of surrender takes us back to the origins of the word "tradition" itself: a giving up, a ceding to authority. But for his readers in 1917, the language of surrender, of self-sacrifice, and continual extinction could not but rephrase the poet's task into a battlefield of creativity—a language that recalls, say, William Noel Hodgson's poem written just before his death at the Battle of the Somme, where he sees his colleagues' "fresh and sanguine sacrifice."[14] Eliot's examples that follow this moment in the essay only add to its anxieties: Dante's Ulysses, Aeschylus's Agamemnon, Shakespeare's Othello. "The difference between art and event," Eliot comments, "is always absolute." But his examples are of artistic imaginings of old war heroes on the way home—lost, killed, or killing. There is a sense throughout "Tradition and the Individual Talent" that, for all Eliot's attempt to escape history itself in favor of a literary past, the historical present remains inescapable. A writer, he averred, "must inevitably be judged by the standards of the past. I say judged, not amputated, by them." How could anyone read such a sentence in 1917 and not smell the battlefield? Even as Eliot finds faith in the literary past, the present keeps returning.

The present keeps returning for us all. It kept returning for Paul Fussell, in his brilliant literary history, *The Great War and Modern Memory* (1975). Fussell here offers an ironic reconsideration of the moralizing tones of the post-Eliotic condition. He argued that the cultural consequence, if not the "meaning" of the First World War lay in the ways in which it came to be inscribed into a broad set of literary archetypes. In its theaters of failed heroism and its romances of unrequited quests, Fussell saw forms of Western narrative. A purple flower, for example, may sprout in Flanders fields; but it sprouts, too, in the imaginations of the critic. Northrop Frye, Fussell notes, "reminds us that [such a flower] 'turns up everywhere in pastoral elegy'" (268). The color "gray" may have filled skies and German uniforms, but it, too, is a marker of particular literary idioms (67), while "ancient tradition associates battle scars with roses" (265). Fussell makes clear that his is a study of how "literary tradition and real life notably transect," and he proposes that, were his book to have had a subtitle, it should be "An Inquiry into the Curious Literariness of Real Life." For soldiers who sat in the trenches with the *Oxford Book of English Verse*, the boundaries between real life and literariness were blurry.

For Fussell—as for Eliot and for a range of critics of the twentieth and early twenty-first century—what matters is less how literature reflects real life than how real life is always imbued with literariness. In the Great War, Fussell had found a story of the literary tradition as a tale of irony: an attempt to find in crafted voice and vision a way of coping with the modern estrangement of language from meaning. Wartime language was euphemistic, allegorical, or just plain lying. Such was the language of modernity itself, and the traditions of war writing—from David Jones through Norman Mailer to Michael Herr and Anthony Swofford—show how the soldier constantly confronts the growing distance between the word and reality. George Orwell had argued this point, too, in his famous "Politics and the English Language," where he illustrates how the idioms of the totalitarian state estrange themselves from fact. For people reared on such suspicions of authoritative language or the reverence for the past, can there be meaning in a literary tradition? In the revised edition of his book, published in 2000, Fussell lamented that we had given up not just on present meaning but also on past example. "The last twenty-five years," he wrote in the postscript to that new edition, "have seen the English literary tradition grow increasingly irrelevant."[15]

Has it? Robert Pinsky, in a book contemporary with Fussell's, argued for the life of the tradition in contemporary writing. His *Situation of Poetry* (1976) defined a literary tradition as "a climate of implicit expectation and tacit knowledge." As a tradition remains alive, he argued, "it changes and grows, and much of the growth consists of extending principles further in their logical directions." Thus, a writer may eschew tradition or react against it: as Pinsky claims, "some conventions operate most clearly when they are violated or discarded."[16]

The tradition may be thought of not as a collection of revered works but rather as a set of practices or habits that constitute the ways in which a culture sees its figurative forms. Twenty-first-century writers and readers may seem to have little use for the "tradition" in an *Oxford Book of English Verse* sense of that term. But there is always a past behind the present, always a template against which the innovative may take shape. Tradition lives not through slavish imitation but through error, mistake, twist, and turn. As the editors of the recent encyclopedic volume, *The Classical Tradition* (2010), have noted, it is the "misunderstandings" of the past, often far more than their scholarly fidelity, that shape their present meaning: "it has often been creative misunderstandings that have preserved the ancient heritage and made it useful for later needs." A student opening this volume to its panoply of color illustrations will find such creative manipulations central to the history of Western art and politics: the learned men in a painting by Sir Joshua Reynolds ape the poses of an ancient fresco; George Washington becomes a figure out of Cicero; and Paul Gauguin, enisled in Tahiti, can model his "Man With an Adze" against the heroes of the Parthenon frieze.[17]

It would be little more than commonplace (or common sense) to say that tradition is no absolute but that it lives, like so many other concepts, as a relational term. Tradition thrives among the non-traditional. But it is more than commonplace to see tradition as the loam from which originality itself must spring. At the close of the nineteenth-century,

Paul Valery offered, in his "Letter About Mallarmé," the insight that "We say that an author is original when we cannot trace the hidden transformation that others underwent in his mind; we mean to say that the dependence of what he does on what others have done is excessively complex and irregular."[18] Literary textuality goes on within a system of reading and writing. Originality is not a break with the past as much as it is a transformation of that past—a transformation that may occlude the very pastness of the stimuli for writing. Edward Said, in his *Beginnings* of 1975, opens with Valery's intuition to argue that every act of literary making must set out to discriminate the present from the past. A beginning, he announces, is the "point at which, in a given work, the writer departs from all other works; a beginning immediately establishes relationships with works already existing, relationships of either continuity or antagonism or some mixture of both."[19]

For the Said of the 1970s, the literary beginning served as a fulcrum on which he could balance the new fascinations with the theoretics of the text: the effacement of authorship for textuality, the sense of writing as a kind of "self-estrangement from speech," the sense that a literary text is "neither . . . a 'creative' masterpiece nor a fact of nature but . . . something whose *beginning* condition, irreducibly, is that *it must always be produced, constantly.*"[20] By collapsing the writer's "career" into the text, and by defining the tradition as a body of writings rather than a set of writers, Said and his contemporaries set the stage for further theoretical assumptions about literary authority and originality. It is only a short step from Said's recasting of traditional textual criticism ("since there can be no absolutely correct and 'original' text firmly anchoring subsequent transcriptions in reality, all texts existing in a constantly moving tangle of imagination and error") to the social criticism of Judith Butler in the 1990s. There were no "originals," only copies of copies. No absolute, essential meaning could be found in language or in gender or in race or class. Such phenomena were performances, played out according to conventional social scripts or expectations.[21]

For theoretically minded academics of the last years of the twentieth and the first years of the twenty-first century, such seemingly relativistic positions had little room for "tradition," let alone for individual talent. In the decoupling of the signifier from the signified, in the idea of the self-referentiality of language, in the move of humanistic inquiry away from artifacts of aesthetic appreciation to the discourses and constitutive practices in which such artifacts gained cultural value—in all these intellectual and institutional activities, the idea of tradition seems to have lost out. Said anticipated such moves in *Beginnings*, when he illustrated how the techniques of textual editing wind up, actually, not with an "original" and its copies, but rather only with copies of copies, narratives of slips, mistakes, and iterations of error.

It is this loss of *origin* in modern literary theory that makes the idea of a recuperative, illuminating tradition so difficult. That difficulty, that sense of loss, informs a recent fascination with tradition, once again, in academic and popular criticism. New techniques of formal, verbal analysis have sought to distinguish "literature" from mere "writing." Journalistic criticism has iterated its impatience with the (often caricatured) penchant of the academic for blurring the lines among the great, the good, and the so-so. College curricula, after years of diversifying and expanding, are returning, here and there, to authors, periods, and genres. Professional organizations from the Modern Language Association of America to the English Association of Great Britain now sponsor conferences with almost as many panels about teaching as about scholarship—as if a new faith in teaching could bring back the verities of form and genre, author and period. This emphasis on teaching is an emphasis not simply on curriculum but on the personality of teachers. It trades on the conviction that personal response demands a personal guide. Thus, for many, the social mission of instruction in the skills of writing, reasoning, and rhetoric is inseparable from the face-to-face experience of wonder (a point I will develop at greater length in my final chapter).

Some have sought to resolve the "crisis in the Humanities" by trying to restore a reverence for the great books and the mechanisms of the social order inscribed in a recuperative idea of tradition: reading as a social good, literature as offering the site of personal growth, life as one big book club. *How Proust Can Change Your Life*; *My Life in Middlemarch*; *Reading the OED: One Man One Year*—books such as these proliferate, as if to show us that the history of reading is a personal history; as if the life lived is but a refraction of the life read.[22] That moment in Charles Dickens' *David Copperfield*—when the book's hero finds himself (in all senses of that phrase) in his late father's library—has morphed into a manifesto for the modern literate:

> This was my only and my constant comfort. When I think of it, the picture always rises in my mind, of a summer evening, the boys at play in the churchyard, and I sitting on my bed, reading as if for life.[23]

"Reading as if for life." The philosopher Martha Nussbaum exemplifies a recent trend in social commentary by appropriating this passage as a "wonderful" lesson for the modern reader. "People," she avers, "care for the books they read; and they are changed by what they care for." But, she claims, "Professional writers about literature too often end up losing contact with the love of books," and "once that delight is lost, little remains."[24]

These days, it seems, everyone wants to profess a delight in books. Journalists and reviewers have continued to avow the personal and social good of reading.[25] Academic critics long associated with high theory have averred their continued love of literature, their personal favorites, and their pleasure in the acts of reading and teaching. Jonathan Culler, the Cornell professor whose *Structuralist Poetics* of 1975 and whose advocacy of deconstruction throughout the 1980s and 90s set the tone for two generations of graduate students, has most recently returned to poems that he loves.[26] His *Theory of the Lyric* (2015) explicitly offers no new or revelatory engagements with old texts:

> The study of literature has for some time championed the production of more intricate, more sophisticated, more complex interpretations of literary works. Much of the criticism that results is of great interest, but I have found it gratifying to turn aside from such aims. Here I do not aim to complicate but rather to focus on some of the most appealing poems of the Western lyric tradition without presuming to develop new interpretations: registering the sorts of pleasures they offer, highlighting the strangeness of their linguistic acts, identifying their distinctive rhetorical strategies, and trying to offer some account of the range of historical possibilities that they make available.[27]

Notice his language here: gratifying, appealing, Western tradition, pleasures, highlighting, strangeness, possibilities. This is not the language of the late twentieth-century theorist, and certainly not the tone of the college critic caricatured, by Harold Bloom, as a member of the "school of resentment."[28] This is the language of a reader unashamedly telling us what he likes, and the book that follows these remarks explains why he likes it and how he can help you like it too.

All of this language is the language of *loving literature,* and Deirdre Lynch's recent book of that title illuminates the history of affective attachment to the book and to the act of reading. A scholar of the eighteenth century, Lynch finds in her chosen period the origins, not so much of the professional practice of literary scholarship as the social idiom of literary desire. "British culture," she argues, "came to accede to an arrangement...that had literature become available to readers first and foremost as private, passional persons rather than as members of a rational, civic-minded public."[29] It is this individual relationship to books that Lynch finds both as social history and as fictional narrative. For what she finds inscribed in the fictions that we read are the ideals of literate desire and fulfillment that had brought us to the book in the first place. Reading, in Lynch's narrative, becomes an act of friendship, of domestication, of care, and of love.

Together with many other recent studies, Lynch's book represents a new turn in the critical assessment of a felt relationship to literary making. They signal that an understanding of tradition should no longer be an exercise in elite belonging, but, instead, an experiment in finding ourselves in a (sometimes friendly, sometimes unfriendly) past. My own book here offers a vision of tradition as a shaping of the writing and the reading life. The traditions of book making (physical acts of writing, printing, binding, selling) are as much about literary history as the traditions of the sonnet, or the novel, or the epic. The traditions of critical analysis contribute equally to literary history, and part of my argument is that the late-twentieth- and early-twenty-first-century fascination with a revival of philology is an attempt to ground the practices of teaching and criticism in a tradition based on knowledge and judgment.

In order to explore that relationship of knowledge and judgment to the institutions of instruction and order, I turn to a set of related concepts that have long governed debates in literary study. All of these concepts have been redefined since the pedagogues of classical antiquity made Homer and Virgil the core documents of literate education in the West. Matters of canon, imitation, representation, and cultural politics have been the axes along which men and women have read and written. I take on each one to review some of their challenges for a new reassessment of tradition in our literary practice.

Canon

Our word comes from an older theological vocabulary. The Greek word *kanon* meant a measuring rod, and modern scholars trace its application in biblical studies back to Roman Judaism and early Christianity. Establishing the rightful contents and the order of the Old and New Testaments shaped a sense of shared belonging. Belief became a matter of textual affiliation. The idea of a religion of the book— whether it be Judaism, Christianity, or Islam—necessarily implies a link between literacy and devotion. Though the word *canon* was not used, in English, in this way until the later eighteenth century, the concept was clear throughout the West, and it inflected notions of selection for both secular and sacred writings. The medieval idea of the *auctores*—that collection of authoritative writings and writers— centered on establishing what was authentic and what was spurious. There was a clear sense that there were some books more important than others, and some writers necessary for everyone to know.[30]

During the Anglo-Saxon period in England, King Alfred the Great inaugurated a program of textual production and translation, keyed to turning certain works of Latin into the vernacular. As he put it in his prefatory letter to the translation of Gregory the Great's *Pastoral Care*, there are certain books "necessary for all men to know." Among those books that survive from this period are Old English translations of Boethius's *Consolation of Philosophy* and St. Augustine's *Soliloquies*. These are texts not just of late classical wisdom or of early Christian doctrine. They are texts that reflect on the nature of learning itself, with dramatized figures of instruction, injunctions to good reading and good listening, and arguments for what we might call a spiritual literacy in reading the world.[31]

What made these books necessary—what makes any book or collection of books necessary—lies less in the absolute content of individual works than in their shared participation in a system of values. King Alfred's values, as he stated in the prefatory letter to the

Pastoral Care, were those of wisdom, learning, and literacy in both Latin and the vernacular. Other canons at other times had different criteria of selection. The critic John Guillory, in the late 1980s and early 90s, formulated a conception of the canon as a set of social values that helps explain these varying historical selections. No single work, he wrote, is canonical. "Canonicity," he argued, "is not the property of the work itself but of its transmission, its relation to other works in a collocation of works."[32] Whatever the practical implications of Guillory's formulation, its theoretical foundations were clear. Meaning in a literary system, much like meaning in a linguistic or a social system, was not essential but relational. Texts, signs, or practices are meaningful within a collection.

What does such a relational theory of meaning do to and with "tradition"? The canonicity of certain works, in arguments for literary tradition or traditionalism, has largely been made on essentialist, rather than relational, criteria. Thus F. R. Leavis, in his *Great Tradition,* could assemble a collection of books and authors valuable for what they absolutely were. Criteria of "greatness" grew out of an understanding of a writer's verbal technique, social purpose, and cultural longevity. There was a sense of moral import to these great novels. Conrad, Austen, Eliot, and James "change the possibilities of art for practitioners and readers," and foster "an awareness of the possibilities of life."[33]

Leavis himself never used the word "canon" in *The Great Tradition.* But the idea of the canon is everywhere in the book, with the criteria of canonicity (what Leavis called "greatness") to be a level of "formal perfection...that can be appreciated only in terms of the moral preoccupations that characterize the novelist's particular interest in life." Leavis makes many comparisons throughout his argument—some writers are better than others, some more entertaining, some more deft in their verbal technique—but his clutch of great writers remains stable. Thus, while acknowledging the "genius" of Dickens, he cannot rank him among the greats because his "genius was that of a great entertainer, and he had for the most part no profounder responsibility as a creative artist than this description suggests."[34]

Reading Leavis seventy years on, we can surely find what Guillory would call his system of values at work. We can recognize that, for all his claims for essential quality, Leavis's argument is one of judgments.

He expresses a sensibility rather than a body of knowledge, and that, it seems to me, is one of the key distinctions for a study of tradition and its canons.

For the job of reading, as Leavis implies, is the cultivation of a particular sensibility on the part of the reader. Developing that sensibility enables critical judgment and aesthetic appreciation. It also enables moral instruction. Leavis seems largely unconcerned with knowledge as a centerpiece of literary study. His work spends little time excavating the societal or economic or political specifics of the periods from Austen to Conrad and James. He spends almost no time with authorial biography. He appears unaware (or just uninterested) in the relationship of literary culture to the material production of books: George Eliot's habits of proofreading and revising, James's penchant for dictation and his preference for the sound of a particular typewriter, the fact that Conrad did not even learn English until his twenties, and so on. The center point of Leavis's idea of both tradition and of greatness is this inner sensibility, gifted, but also honed in practice. The experience of reading becomes an engagement, therefore, between sensibilities—those of the reader and the author. Grounded in this world, the primary task of the critic is "discrimination."

Leavis has long been seen as something of an outlier in the traditions of modern criticism. Yet, his arguments do stand at the heart of a long-standing debate on the nature of reading and teaching and, in turn, on the question of whether literary study should be the cultivation of a sensibility or the acquisition of knowledge. Such a debate has informed matters of literary history for centuries, and they matter equally for an early-twenty-first century classroom and commons.

Taste and Knowledge

The modern history of literary study sits on the axes of knowledge and sensibility.[35] John Locke, in his *Essay Concerning Human Understanding* of 1690, developed what would become the Empiricist notion of learning as a product of sense perception. Denying the conception of "innate ideas" (that we are born with things or notions in our mind), Locke saw the process of learning as a process of garnering information about the world through the sensory engagement with particulars. Sense and sensibility thus grounded the process by which human beings make meaning out of the world. They grounded, too, the process by which human beings make meaning out of literary and artistic objects. As Denise Gigante has shown in her *Taste: A Literary History* (2005), this Lockean empiricism gave rise to what eighteenth-century writers would call the "man of taste." For Samuel Johnson, taste in all its forms—experiencing literature and art, as well as food and drink—became (in Gigante's words) an experience of "social communion" (8). The cultivation of taste emerged, then, out of a mix of philosophical and social views, balancing "on the border between aesthetics and consumerism" (14).

Taste may have been an intellectual and cultural phenomenon, but it was also an etymological one. The multiple connotations of the word itself grew out of its own history, and one of the great word-plays from the classical to the early modern period lay in the Latin word *savor*. Originally meaning both taste and knowledge, the word provoked writers to see learning as a form of ingestion. The bee gathered nectar to make honey as the reader gathered texts to make knowledge. This simile (famous from Roman antiquity on) yoked together these two senses of the word. Writers could play on *savor*, *savoir*, *sapor*, and so on. John Milton, in a characteristic display of linguistic erudition, has Adam say to Eve, upon his eating of the Apple in *Paradise Lost*, "Eve, now I see thou art exact of taste," making clear this fundamental association between forbidden knowing and forbidden tasting.

Nineteenth-century academic historicism and positivism sought to change all this. The goal of literary study came to mean the acquisition of knowledge itself—not to articulate a sensibility but to describe the literary object in the world. In the study of language, for example, the development of Indo-European philology was designed to make word histories grounded in the histories and relationships of their sounds. Etymology became (by and large) the study of historical phonology. The history of a word could thus be reconstructed by comparing forms from surviving or recorded languages. This comparative method was a far cry from older, so-called "metaphysical" etymologies. From the Middle Ages on, there was a penchant for finding an essential meaning in a word. Wood burns, an argument went, because the Latin word "ignis" inheres already in the Latin word "lignis." Such reasoning, perfectly acceptable for a millennium, was rendered ludicrous by the Victorian philologists.[36]

It was this turn in language study that inflected a historical, knowledge-based turn to literary study. The editing of texts came to be understood as a scientific process. Comparative philology provided the model for comparative textual criticism: setting differing texts of the same work side-by-side in order to reconstruct a putative authorial original. It became the model, too, for comparative physiology, and with the arguments of Darwin gaining acceptance by the end of the nineteenth century, the comparative method in anatomy enabled physiologists to reconstruct earlier biological forms.[37] The language tree—with Indo-European at the base and modern languages at the branches—was adapted to the tree of life, with progressively more and more "primitive" genera and classes moving down the trunk.

Knowledge came to be understood as both empirical and historical. It was not simply an aggregation of facts or data, but the placing of that data in a larger narrative of development. Literary history itself came to be seen as such a narrative. From the Chaucerian Middle Ages, through Shakespeare, Milton, the Romantics, and beyond, the story of literature in the vernacular was written as a story of development: a historical narrative of authors, forms, and languages. The canon of literature for the late nineteenth century emerged, therefore, not just out of likes and dislikes, but out of the place of particular works in a historical narrative of literary development and inheritance.

This process was not simply intellectual but ethical. It offered up a new light on knowledge; indeed, it made the acquisition of historical, linguistic knowledge a marker of social and professional accomplishment. Holger Pedersen in the 1920s praised the comparative philological method in these highly judgmental terms: "It was the establishment of this fundamental principle in method which pulled etymological scholarship out of the bog where it had stuck fast since classical times, and rendered the existence of comparative linguistics possible."[38] Compare his phrasing with that of Edmund Gosse, cited in the *OED*: "They were all engaged with keeping bright, and handing on unquenched, the torch of literary tradition." In these idioms of illumination, of pulling language study from the dark bog of the past or in lighting torches of tradition, we can see the interplay of knowledge and taste, fact and judgment.

The legacy of the Victorian philologists and positivists was not simply the elimination of personal taste or sensibility as a criterion of value. It was the relocation of that value in a historical narrative, a framing of the philological together with the literary. Canons of writers became canons of usage. One legacy of this philology was to make literary canonicity a matter of linguistic innovation: a narrative of writers such as Chaucer, Spenser, Shakespeare, Milton, Wordsworth, Austen, Dickens, Scott, George Eliot, Twain, and so on, each one defined by how he or she brought new words into literary usage, took syntax and made it into a style, and codified colloquial speech into formal writing.

I will make much more of this argument in later chapters, as I look at the traditions of philology and the relationships of literary and linguistic knowledge-making in the histories of scholarship. For now, I want to call attention to the notion that the difference between taste and knowledge is that the former is static and the latter is dynamic. Taste is something acquired, cultivated, and maintained, but once you have it, you have it. Knowledge, however, is something continually accreted.

But what constitutes "originality" in more recent critical and academic study has been contested. At stake is not just whether anyone had found or thought what you had found or thought. At stake was the idea of whether anything at all could be original: whether the world was made of copies, and what the place of imitation was in shaping the discourses of discovery.

Imitation and Originality

The traditions of instruction in the West grounded themselves in imitation. Learning grew out of copying the masters.[39] Literature hewed to pre-established forms and genres; rhetorical tropes and techniques could be learned and practiced; allusions to previous authors marked the erudition of the current writer. Literary education keyed itself, in these traditions, to memorization and recitation. Perhaps the most famous examples from the late classical period appear in St. Augustine's *Confessions*, when he recalls how, as a schoolboy, he was made to memorize the wanderings of Aeneas and the laments of Dido, and how he was called upon to recite Juno's speech from the opening of the *Aeneid* and bits of Terence's comedies. Augustine, of course, builds his narrative of personal development out of a synthesis of Christian salvation and classical epic. Carthage and Rome may be sites in the geography of his growth; but they are also locales of the Virgilian imagination. So, too, through his rich sequence of quotation and allusion to the scriptures, especially to the Psalms, Augustine creates an original narrative of individual development through the words of a recalled textual canon.[40]

Such techniques filled the range of writings from the late antique through early modern periods. Templates of longing—Virgil's *Aeneid*, Boethius's *Consolation of Philosophy*, Old and New Testament narratives— generated works of powerful vernacularity that held in brilliant tension the allusive and the personal. We treasure, for example, Chaucer for his seeming originality, his realism, and his prescient ironies. And yet, he presents his own task as one of compiling and translating, never claiming that he had truly deviated from the past paths.

What did it mean to be "original" in such a practice? Did it mean simply to deviate from the model, or was it something more complex? The scholar G. W. Pigman, III, has discerned, throughout the classical and early modern periods, "an open struggle with the model for preeminence, a struggle in which the model must be recognized to assure the text's victory" (4). This agonistic sense of literary history is nowhere more apparent than in the most canonical of English literary writers. Chaucer presents his *Troilus and Criseyde* as a translation from an old original—and yet, he deflects our attention from that real original, Boccaccio's *Filostrato*, by inventing a bogus source author, Lollius, and never mentioning Boccaccio by name (indeed, Boccaccio was one of Chaucer's most fertile sources and models, and while Chaucer acknowledges just about every writer from antiquity to his present, from Homer to Petrarch, he never once mentions Boccaccio). The model must be recognized, but it must be occluded. Such was Spenser's strategy throughout the *Fairie Queene*, and such is Milton's in *Paradise Lost*, where in Book II, Satan's journey through darkness models itself on the Spenserian, allegorical quest—only to move beyond it and, in the process, reject the old romances for new epic.

This sense of a struggle resonates with many other, more contemporary literary theories. Edward Said, as I already have noted, argued that each beginning establishes the writer in a relationship of continuity or antagonism with the writings that have gone before. In Harold

Bloom's sense of an "anxiety of influence" what he dubbed "strong" writers challenge and overcome their literary forbears to create new versions of old forms.[41]

But, as I have already mentioned, such systems of literary history presuppose the idea not just of originality but origin. The literary theory of the late twentieth century made the distinction between copy and original illusory. What did the writer represent: a world, a text, a meaning? The late-twentieth-century move from structuralism to post-structuralism largely argued that language did not represent the world, but rather that it represented language. The system of representation was not mimetic but self-referential. Signs were estranged from the things they signified. We were copies of copies. Identity was a performance.

Such a position had a profound impact, not only on the study of verbal artifacts but of individual identity. The work of Judith Butler, in particular, codified this position into a political, as well as academic, principle. "Gender," she famously wrote, "is a kind of imitation for which there is no original; in fact it is a kind of imitation that produces the very notion of the original as an effect and consequence of the imitation itself."[42] Implicit in this sense of gender as a social performance, rather than an essential quality, is a broader questioning of all forms of performed behavior, including language. Has everything that can be said already been said? Can there be nothing that is truly literal, but are all linguistic expressions really, in the end, all figurative (such a view, it should be pointed out, reaches back to Romantic notions of language, recuperated and rephrased in the traditions of deconstruction)? Such views have implications not only for gender but for race. The word "signifyin'" in the Afro-American traditions connoted the practice of re-speaking the words of the powerful by the mouths of the powerless.[43] Even if the words were exactly the same, the context, meaning, and value of the utterance changed, depending on the status of the speaker.

For readers, writers, and teachers in the early twenty-first century, is it, then, possible to be original? Is our current condition one of repetition and quotation? Given these broad theoretical and cultural predispositions, how can we not (it might well be asked) maintain an ironic relationship to literary tradition—especially if we see that tradition not as a parade of originals but rather as a string of simulacra?

Irony and Sincerity

The legacy of literary and cultural theory is a pervasive ironic distancing of the self from acts of valuation. We live in an ironic world—a fact we may lament but which we need to face.

When I was completing my history of *Children's Literature*, I came to see late-twentieth- and early-twenty-first-century childhood as a condition of ironic detachment. I watched my own son (born in 1992) grow up with what seemed as a far-too-great amount of ennui for a pre-teen. I read our books together with a greater sensitivity (if not a soreness) for ironic snark.[44]

Jon Scieska's *Time Warp Trio* books, designed for the precocious tween, brilliantly called attention to the ways in which contemporary irony challenges literary history. At the end of the book, *Summer Reading is Killing Me!* (1998), there is a "Summer Reading List" appended, at first glance something designed for schoolroom or home use. But as we read through, we see something far from straight or straightforward. "Write the title and author of the book," it begins, benignly enough. Then it instructs:

> Tap your pencil on the paper.
> Stare out the window and daydream.
> Put the study guide away and don't look at it again until
>   the night before the first day of school.

What Scieska knows here is that, in a world full of books, nothing comes without irony. His *Time Warp Trio* kids—smart, world-weary New Yorkers—find themselves trapped in historical moments of high culture. Everything has already been said; everything has been quoted. Life in such a world is life in the already uttered, where no statement can be taken at face value and where success comes not just through strength or knowledge but through a streetwise, bullshitty wit.

Scieska's work was, of course not unique: Louis Sachar's *Holes*, Lia Block's Weeziebat books, and tales from Lemony Snicket have schooled two generations of young readers in an idiom of urban disaffection, snide wisdom, and "been there done that" distance. This is the world of "whatever," a blowing-off of the impediments to life. The *OED* notes that the word emerged in the 1970s to connote indifference, skepticism, impatience, or passive acceptance of other people's failures. Again, war seems to have shaped a distance from rhetorical authority, an ironizing of tradition. The first quotation the *OED* presents, from 1973, defines "whatever" in a document from the US Secretary of Defense titled, *To Our Returned Prisoners of War*: "Whatever, equivalent to 'that's what I meant.' Usually implies boredom with topic or lack of concern for a precise definition of meaning." Paul Fussell's *Great War and Modern Memory* is a product of this emerging sensibility, and his fascination with the parodies that soldiers made of their officer's edicts frames post-Edwardian anomie in a post-Vietnam light.

Whatever. How can we love literature in an age of blithe indifference? Have we lost a concern for a precise definition of meaning? Internet searches, Wikipedia, and Google books have only enhanced our sense of distance from a literary past and from an authorial original. Can we trust an encyclopedia whose authors remain anonymous? What does it mean to curl up with a digital scan, rather than with a printed, bound page? These questions bear directly on our sense of tradition and the cultural value of the past. For they reflect a broader mistrust of official language, a suspicion of authoritative claims to value, and a playful lack of seriousness. My teenage mantra, "don't trust anyone over thirty," morphed into the axiom of the *X-Files* of the 1990s, "trust no one," and the sense, now, not to even trust yourself. The rise of so-called "fictional" autobiographies bears eloquent witness to this phenomenon, as does the overarching debate about whether any memoir can be factual or true.[45] A minor industry has grown up to debunk personal narratives of survival, recovery, or sanctity. Is anything true? Do we care? The novelist Wright Morris averred, in a statement quoted with approval by Paul Fussell, "Anything processed by memory is fiction." Should we acknowledge the deep interplay of trope with truth, or should we just throw up our hands? Whatever.

For the past decade, the editors of the *Oxford English Dictionary* have crowned a "word of the year" that seems to codify a cultural position or distill a moment in the interplay of language and society. The 2014 word of the year was *vape*. The word means "to inhale and exhale the vapor produced by an electronic cigarette or similar device." With the widespread public banning of smoking, "vaping" became an acceptable alternative. Vape cafes and vape shops have sprung up in New York, London, and other world cities.

At the heart of this word is *vapor*, the ineffable waft of odor and appearance. An electronic cigarette remains a simulacrum of a cigarette, much as an e-book is a simulacrum of a book. Both deliver, in mechanical ways, something that used to be delivered directly—through type, tobacco, and paper. Both create the illusion of engagement, mediated by technology. The old ways have been recast into what linguists call retronyms: acoustic guitar, tobacco cigarette, snail mail, print books.

Will literature come to us as vape? There seems to be a need, now, for a return to unmediated cultural experience. We want to do things with our books, to love them and to live through them. But can we ever get beyond a cultural suspicion of tradition that lies so much at the heart of critical discourse? Some books, like cigarettes, have been perceived as bad for you. But when you read even the most painful, disturbing, or challenging of texts, you may feel what the critic Richard Klein felt when he lit up: "a darkly beautiful, inevitably painful pleasure that arises from some intimation of eternity." Like a cigarette, a book is "not just an object one holds in one's hand, it must be considered a subject, a creature alive with a body and spirit of its own." Some people may find literature "useless." A recent Stanford University student newspaper issue asked, "Are the Humanities Toxic?" And yet, again, perhaps like cigarettes, it is this uselessness or even toxicity that makes books fascinating, bringing a "sublimely, darkly beautiful pleasure to the lives" of readers.[46]

My goal here is to walk the tightrope: to argue for a meaningful relationship to literary tradition while at the same time remaining aware of our cultural condition of ironic distance. We can have a felt response to literature, while acknowledging that such a response always, throughout history, came in mediated form. Literature does not exist without its media of transmission. Handwritten manuscripts, printed books, and pixelated screens are the bearers of literacy. Blackboards and whiteboards, tables and chairs, windows and screens are the sites of teaching. My book takes a distinctively professional and personal approach to understanding literary tradition. And if it shies away from embracing, in full, a notion of tradition as an "unquenched torch," it does not see it purely as the simulacrum of a Kindle. Light up. Inhale.

Notes

1. Lionel Trilling, "The Sense of the Past," *The Partisan Review*, May–June 1942, reprinted in *The Liberal Imagination: Essays on Literature and Society* (New York: Harcourt, 1950; rpt. New York: New York Review Books, 2008), 181.

2. See Raymond Williams, *Culture and Society, 1780–1850* (London: Chatto & Windus, 1958); Chris Baldick, *The Social Mission of English Criticism, 1848–1932* (Oxford: Oxford University Press, 1983); Gerald Graff, *Professing Literature: An Institutional History* (Chicago: University of Chicago Press, 1989); John Guillory, *Cultural Capital: The Problem of Literary Canon Formation* (Chicago: University of Chicago Press, 1995); Jonathan Kramnick, *Making the English Canon: Print-Capitalism and the Cultural Past, 1700–1770* (Cambridge: Cambridge University Press, 1998); Seth Lerer, *Error and the Academic Self: The Scholarly Imagination, Medieval to Modern* (New York: Columbia University Press); Deirdre Shauna Lynch, *Loving Literature: A Cultural History* (Chicago: University of Chicago Press, 2015).

3. All references to the *Oxford English Dictionary* (*OED*) are to the currently updated online edition, www.oed.com.

4. Edmund Gosse, *Collected Essays of Edmund Gosse: Portraits and Sketches* (London: Heinemann, 1913), viii.

5. See D. J. Palmer, *The Rise of English Studies* (London: Oxford University Press, 1965); Baldick, *Social Mission*; Graff, *Professing Literature*; Hayden White, *Metahistory: The Historical Imagination in Nineteenth-Century Europe* (Baltimore: Johns Hopkins University Press, 1973).

6. From "Kipling," originally published in *The Nation*, October 17, 1943, and reprinted in *The Liberal Imagination*; this quotation from 127.

7. Trilling, *Liberal Imagination*,185.

8. Louis Menand, "Introduction," *The Liberal Imagination*, xi.

9. See James Gleick, *The Information: A History, A Theory, A Flood* (New York: Pantheon, 2011); Andrew Piper, *Book Was There: Reading in Electronic Times* (Chicago: University of Chicago Press, 2012).

10. T. S. Eliot, *Selected Essays*, 2nd edition (London: Faber & Faber, 1934).

11. Eliot, *Selected Essays*, 14.

12. See Graff, *Professing Literature*, and Roland Greene, "Close Reading Transformed: The New Criticism and the World," in Nina S. Levine and David Lee Miller, eds, *A Touch More Rare: Harry Berger, Jr. and the Art of Interpretation* (New York: Fordham University Press, 2009), 115–24.

13. Eliot, *Selected Essays*, 17.

14. William Noel Hodgson, "Before Action," quoted in Paul Fussell, *The Great War and Modern Memory* (New York: Oxford University Press, 1975), 67. For a different reading of these idioms and images, see Jewel Spears Brooker, "Writing the Self: Dialectic and Impersonality in T. S. Eliot," in Giovanni Cianci and Jason Harding, eds, *T. S. Eliot and the Concept of Tradition* (Cambridge: Cambridge University Press, 2007), 41–57.

15. (New York: Oxford University Press, 2000), 369.

16. Robert Pinsky, *The Situation of Poetry: Contemporary Poetry and its Traditions* (Princeton: Princeton University Press, 1976), 3, 5.

17. Anthony Grafton, Glenn W. Most, and Salvatore Settis, *The Classical Tradition* (Cambridge, Mass.: Harvard University Press, 2010), vii, and plates 53, 54.

18. Quoted in Edward Said, *Beginnings: Intention and Method* (Baltimore: Johns Hopkins University Press, 1975), 14–15.

19. Said, *Beginnings*, 3.

20. Said, *Beginnings*, 197, 205, respectively.

21. Judith Butler, *Gender Trouble* (New York: Routledge, 1990).

22. Alain de Botton, *How Proust Can Change Your Life* (New York: Vintage, 1997); Rebecca Mead, *My Life in Middlemarch* (New York: Random House, 2014); Ammon Shea, *Reading the Oxford English Dictionary* (London: Penguin, 2008).

23. Charles Dickens, *The Personal History of David Copperfield* [The Oxford Illustrated Dickens] (Oxford: Oxford University Press, 1989), 56.

24. Martha Nussbaum, *Love's Knowledge: Essays on Philosophy and Literature* (New York: Oxford University Press, 1990), 230–1.

25. Michael Dirda, *A Year of Reading, Collecting, and Living with Books* (New York: Pegasus, 2015); James Wood, *The Nearest Thing to Life* (Waltham, Mass.: Brandeis University Press, 2015); Tim Parks, *Where I'm Reading From: The Changing World of Books* (New York: New York Review Books, 2015).

26. Jonathan Culler, *Structuralist Poetics* (Ithaca: Cornell University Press, 1975); *On Deconstruction: Theory and Criticism after Structuralism* (Ithaca: Cornell University Press, 1982).

27. Jonathan Culler, *Theory of the Lyric* (Cambridge, Mass.: Harvard University Press, 2015), vii.

28. Harold Bloom, *The Western Canon* (New York: Harcourt Brace, 1994), esp. 7, 527.

29. Lynch, *Loving Literature*, 6–7.

30. See Bruce Metzger, *The Canon of the New Testament: Its Origin, Development, and Significance* (Oxford: Oxford University Press, 1997); A. J. Minnis, *Medieval Theory of Authorship* (London: Scolar, 1979).

31. Simon Keynes and Michael Lapidge, *Alfred the Great* (Harmondsworth: Penguin, 1983).

32. John Guillory, "Canonical and Non-Canonical: A Critique of the Debate," *ELH* 54 (1987): 483–527, and *Cultural Capital*. See, too, Richard Terry, *Poetry and the Making of the English Literary Past 1660–1781* (Oxford: Oxford University Press, 2001), esp. 35–62. For a critique of Guillory's equation (and that of many working in his wake) of "the history of cultural capital with the history of the curriculum" and the implications of that equation for the making of canons, see Lynch, *Loving Literature*, 280 n. 13.

33. F. R. Leavis, *The Great Tradition: George Eliot, Henry James, Joseph Conrad* (New York: Doubleday, 1954), 10. For a valuable, brief overview of Leavis and his institutional contexts, see Stephen Heath, "I. A. Richards, F. R. Leavis and Cambridge English," in Richard Mason, ed., *Cambridge Minds* (Cambridge: Cambridge University Press, 1994), 20–33.

34. Leavis, *Great Tradition*, 18, 275, respectively.

35. Material in this paragraph is indebted to Denise Gigante, *Taste: A Literary History* (New Haven: Yale University Press, 2005).

36. See Holger Pedersen, *Linguistic Science in the Nineteenth Century*, trans. John W. Spargo (Cambridge, Mass.: Harvard University Press, 1931); Hans Aarsleff, *The Study of Language in England 1780–1860* (Princeton: Princeton University Press, 1967); Linda Dowling, *Language and Decadence in the Victorian Fin de Siècle* (Princeton: Princeton University Press, 1986); Dennis Taylor, *Hardy's Literary Language and Victorian Philology* (Oxford: Oxford University Press, 1993); Lerer, *Error and the Academic Self*, esp. 103–74.

37. See Stephen G. Alter, *Darwinism and the Linguistic Image* (Baltimore: Johns Hopkins University Press, 2002).

38. Pedersen's book originally appeared in Danish in 1924 and in English in 1931; I quote from Spargo's translation, 240.

39. G. W. Pigman, III, "Versions of Imitation in the Renaissance," *Renaissance Quarterly* 33 (1980): 1–32.

40. St. Augustine, *Confessions*, trans. R. Pine-Coffin (Harmondsworth: Penguin, 1961). For a suggestive set of encounters with Augustine's bookishness, and the implications of his representations of textual and spiritual literacy for modern, "electronic" readers, see Piper, *Book Was There*, 1–7, 14, 113, 122, 133.

41. Harold Bloom, *The Anxiety of Influence: A Theory of Poetry* (New York: Oxford University Press, 1973).

42. Butler, "Imitation and Gender Insubordination," in Diana Fuss, ed., *Inside/Out: Lesbian Theories, Gay Theories* (New York: Routledge, 1991), 21.

43. See Henry L. Gates, Jr., *The Signifying Monkey: A Theory of African-American Literary Criticism* (New York: Oxford University Press, 1988).

44. Material in the following two paragraphs adapts a much longer exposition in *Children's Literature: A Reader's History from Aesop to Harry Potter* (Chicago: University of Chicago Press, 2008), 305–7.

45. See, for example, W. G. Sebald, *The Emigrants*, trans. Michael Hulse (New York: New Directions, 1997); *Austerlitz*, trans. Anthea Bell (New York: Penguin Books, 2002).

46. Richard Klein, *Cigarettes are Sublime* (Durham: Duke University Press, 1993), 3, 10, 17. For the Stanford University debate, see Seth Lerer, "Transformations in the Humanities and Implications for Graduate Education," *Communicator: Council of Graduate Schools* 44:7 (August/September 2011), online at <http://www.cgsnet.org/ckfinder/userfiles/files/comm_2011_08.pdf>.

2

The Copperfield Experience

> Whether I shall turn out to be the hero of my own life, or
> whether that station will be held by anybody else, these pages
> must show. To begin my life with the beginning of my life,
> I record that I was born (as I have been informed and believe) on
> a Friday, at twelve o'clock at night. It was remarked that the
> clock began to strike, and I began to cry, simultaneously. (1)[1]

Thirteen chapters and nearly two hundred pages after this most famous
of novelistic openings, David Copperfield sets out to find himself
again. Rejected by his stepfather and step-aunt, at a loss in London,
and beset by troubles great and small, David resolves to walk to Dover
to find the aunt who had last appeared to him on the evening of his
birth. As if beginning his life anew, he sets out on the road until he
finally finds Betsey Trotwood's house. Unrecognized, of course, by the
woman who had seen him only once, he stumbles. "If you please,
aunt, I am your nephew," and then, bringing her out of shock, he
elaborates: "I am David Copperfield, of Blunderstone, in Suffolk—
when you came, on the night when I was born, and saw my dear
mama" (191). Taking the reader back to the novel's opening sentences,
David presents himself at the moment of his birth. But now, it is not
as the potential hero of his life, but as a boy unhappy, slighted, taught
nothing, run away, and robbed. If the novel had begun with the striking of the clock and the crying of the baby, now it restarts itself, as
language itself breaks down and the boy breaks "into a passion of
crying" (191).

David Copperfield, as its readers, teachers, and critics long have
known, is a novel of such stops and starts, a story told and retold on
the pages of the book of life. It is a story of a writer's growth, a story
of a boy who comes to read the world, himself, and others. David

strives to make linear sense out of the fragments of what appear before him. Gravestone inscriptions, bits of phrasing, and the remains of his late father's library all come together to transform his life into a set of written texts. Long before he sets out for Dover, he takes solace in that library, lost in the great books of his previous century, the canon of adventure tales through which he reimagined his identity, reading, as he put it, "as if for life" (55–6).

I have already called attention to this phrase as a kind of manifesto for the modern literate. The critic Nicholas Dames considers it "an origin myth for literary scholars" and he goes on: "This moment's recurrent presence in criticism can be ascribed to its power to summon up memories of childhood fantasy and the barrier books can build between a vulnerable self and the hostile world."[2] The opening feints of *David Copperfield* mark the reader's and the writer's place in the literary tradition. Just as the boy imagines himself living out the adventures of Roderick Random, or Tom Jones, or Robinson Crusoe, so Dickens's readers are compelled (or manipulated) to imagine themselves on the trajectory of novelistic heroism. The novel's opening pushes us to read ourselves into his potentially heroic shoes, to be heroes of our own lives. The price we pay for living on the page is, at times, being left upon the bookshelf—or, as Dickens himself reflected in his 1850 Preface to the bound edition of the novel, "no one can ever believe this Narrative, in the reading, more than I believed it in the writing."[3]

It is this blurry relationship between reading and writing that I explore in this chapter. *David Copperfield* confronts and newly generates a literary tradition. It frames its narrative against the models of young David's own absorbing reading. But it, too, is a novel of writers as well as readers: David himself, who will grow up to be a novelist, and the extraordinary Mr. Dick, writing his massive and unfinishable Memorial.

For *David Copperfield* has had its afterlife on other writer's bookshelves. Hardly anyone could write a story of growth and education without standing up to Dickens's work. Narrators find themselves in the libraries of ancestors or patrons. They set out to transform their lives into words on a page. They pick and chose among the literary models offered to them and shape their own experience against the other. Like David with his father's books, Jo March in *Little Women* has her epiphanies in her uncle's library: "the wilderness of books in which she could wander where she liked, made the library a region of bliss to her."[4] And she is not alone. Henry Adams records a comparable experience in his *Education*.[5] Esther Forbes's has her young hero recuperate in the library of the Lorne family in *Johnny Tremain*.[6] And in Francois Truffaut's film adaptation of Bradbury's *Fahrenheit 451*, the fireman Montag secretly pulls a copy of *David Copperfield* itself out of its hiding place and traces Dickens's words with insecure fingers: "Whether I shall turn out to be the hero of my own life...."

Dickens set the template for the modern novel of education, cultivation, and self-understanding. *David Copperfield* locates the library in the making of a first-person, author narrator, and it provides a model for later fictions of authorial or artistic development. It continues to inspire: V. S. Naipaul, Derek Walcott, Orhan Pamuk, and Amitav Ghosh are but a few of the world Anglophone writers who frame their narratives of early reading—an ancestor's library, a personal retreat, a private canon of great books—in terms that hearken back to Dickens's David. As Ankhi Mukherjee has shown, such writers tell tales of creating their "own private English literary anthology," as they recount their moral and their literary growth through acts of "self-archiving." Naipaul put it, in his reminiscence of his twelve-year-old self: "literature had given me the wish" to become a writer. Ghosh recalls his own "grandfather's bookcase," full of nineteenth- and twentieth-century novels that testified to "a form of artistic expression that embodies differences in places and culture, emotion and aspiration."[7]

It would be tempting, at this point, to meditate on the broader colonial and post-colonial impact of Dickens on the Anglophone imagination. And later in this chapter, I explore some ways in which Salman Rushdie's *Midnight's Children* responds to and recasts *David Copperfield*'s turns and tropes. The argument I make, however, is less one of politics than personality. The "Copperfield Experience" compels all of us to create archives of the self, to frame a life against our own private English literary anthology. None of us, now, is a nineteenth-century reader; all of us are, in some way or another, estranged from Dickens's metropolitan realism, his institutional imaginations, and his city and his country roads. We can only imagine ourselves in what Edward Said once called the "outlying spaces of deviation and uncertainty" that Dickens saw.[8]

This is my point. We come, today, to *David Copperfield* (as we may come to nearly all constituents of the literary canon) through a history of reflection and reminiscence, classroom, and critique. We can love and revere such books and, at the same time, work through the ironies and ideologies that are embedded in their texts and that have mediated them to us. The Copperfield experience of sitting in a library and building up that "barrier" between imagination and the world is one that we can still have, but with self-awareness and reflection. Maybe we should think of this less as a barrier than as a stimulus. As David himself says, "they kept alive my fancy, and my hope of something beyond that place and time." We read Dickens, as we read the tradition, to keep alive our hope of something beyond place and time.

Such an approach requires a level of "close reading" that has come under challenge, lately, from the academic mandarin. The intimate and attentive life that David has in books no longer chimes with one of the most challenging developments in literary study in the first years of the twenty-first century. Franco Moretti has called it "distant reading": the study of literary works not as verbal artifacts but as markers in the social exchange of taste and knowledge.[9] Distant reading asks us not to engage with tradition as a narrative of art but to develop a set of "visualization tools" that transform literary history into "a set of two-dimensional signs that can be grasped at a single glance."[10] Graphs, maps, and trees displace the essay or the explication as the means of understanding literature in its social context. To read the Victorian novel "distantly" is not so much to pay attention to an individual book's key words, than it is to chart such words across the corpus of novels, aided by tools of data mining. Distant reading takes us outside of the house of fiction at street level and enables us, in effect, to see architectures of imagination from above.

Both close and distant reading find their actions dramatized in *David Copperfield*. Their tensions provide us with a road map for our own critical positions. And on that map, I circle back to the remarkable Mr. Dick. He is, in many ways, the quintessentially Dickensian character: suddenly great, suddenly small, at times divine, at times a fool.

"Grey-haired and florid," brilliantly lucid and theatrically opaque, Mr. Dick makes his appearance at Aunt Betsey's as, at first, but one more brilliant social caricature. Some have found him a madman;

others see him as autistic or schizophrenic. His is, however, not a medical but a literary condition. Constantly writing his own endless memoirs, obsessed with the severed head of King Charles I, taking his pages and turning them into high-flying kites, Mr. Dick evokes an alternative way of writing the world. For, if David's job is to create a coherent narrative on the page, Mr. Dick's is to offer a set of fragments flown into the air.

He represents a different way of living with the traditions of literature, the novel, and the realist representation of the self. When he appears, seemingly daft but actually quite deft, he is no character out of past life but out of an imagined future. I take this character from *David Copperfield* as a prescient figure for ourselves: an invitation to engage (perhaps even to indulge) our postmodern preoccupations with the partial, the pastiche, and the endlessly postponed. His is a literacy of fragments, a world of writing without end, of readers who exist not in the bookshop or the library but in the very air.

I.

Mr. Dick may have many problems, but one that stands out is his arresting inability to separate his own life from what he has read. A highly curated literary tradition (the story of the Interregnum, of the King's beheading, of the historiography of rule and reason) has made his self-narration impossible. But, as with so much in the novel and with so much in our own lives, we cannot escape the affect of the reader. For all of Mr. Dick's seemingly postmodern fragmentation, there is joy here: joy for him, for David, and for myself. Our acts of loving literature occur even in the weirdest of places. What gives pleasure in this book is the vertiginous thrill of just barely losing oneself in the text, of barely controlling the flying kite with a thin line, of recognizing that lives make themselves of fragments in need of assembly. I can read closely and distantly, personally and professionally, lovingly and critically. That is what *David Copperfield* teaches me how to do.

Dickens, it has been claimed, anticipated much. Joyce's city, Beckett's wilderness, Kafka's dread, Proust's remembrance, the cinema, the Internet—we find their seeds not just in *David Copperfield*, but in *Bleak House, Great Expectations, Little Dorrit, Our Mutual Friend*, and elsewhere.[11] The critic Jay Clayton found Dickens in cyberspace, intuiting in nineteenth-century systems of knowledge-building and communication premonitions of our present.[12] In Mr. Dick, we see the seeds of a postmodernist imagination, the eternal copyist, keeping the past at bay through constant writing. Young Copperfield comes to him, it seems, as if a schoolboy, reared on Defoe, Swift, and Cervantes, were to have an office hour with David Foster Wallace.

Mr. Dick also offers up a test case for Leah Price's recent claims about Victorian literary culture: a culture of doing things not just with but *to* books, a culture that took texts as objects of social absorption and of physical manipulation. Price has made much of what she calls the "absorptive" quality of reading throughout Dickens—the ways in which his characters will find, and lose, themselves in acts of reading. Dickens's characters, in Price's account, seek to make sense of life through acts of literate interpretation.[13] For Mr. Dick, reading as if for life does not mean sitting in a room but running along hills, flying inscribed kites.

His true name is Mr. Richard Babley, but he cannot bear to be addressed by it. "You think Mr. Dick a short name, eh?" Betsey asks David, and David agrees. But against the brevity of his moniker, he is at work on what appears to be a monster of a Memorial, an incoherent story of his life as babbling as his given name implies. It grows out of a loss and hurt, and readers have long found him a foil for both Dickens's and David's literary ministrations. As Stanley Tick had put it, in an incisive and still influential essay almost half-a-century ago, "in a novel deeply infused with autobiographical data...we must pay the utmost attention to a character whose sole occupation is the self-imposed task of writing his autobiography." Mr. Dick has, in Tick's words, "a metaphorical function in the novel," one that looks back upon the author's own attempts to balance fiction against lived experience, the formal strictures of a verbal craft against the sprawl of life itself.[14] And at the end, Mr. Dick's own last words echo for us still: "He greets me rapturously," David recalls, "and whispers, with many winks, 'Trotwood, you will be glad to hear that I shall finish the Memorial when I have nothing else to do.'" But, long before this moment, he had much to do. When David goes upstairs to fetch him, early in his days with Aunt Betsey, he finds a man absorbed in the rapture of writing:

> Thinking, as I went, that if Mr. Dick had been working at his
> Memorial long, at the same rate as I had seen him working

at it, through the open door, when I came down, he was probably getting on very well indeed. I found him still driving at it with a long pen, and his head almost laid upon the paper. He was so intent upon it that I had ample leisure to observe the large paper kite in a corner, the confusion of bundles of manuscript, the number of pens, and above all, the quantity of ink (which he seemed to have in, in half-gallon jars by the dozen), before he observed my being present.

It takes but little stretch to see, in Mr. Dick, a half-baked Dickens, short of name, but long of pen and full of ink.[15] As we read on, we see him writing his Memorial, obsessively recording something about King Charles I, pasting his sheets onto his kite, flying his words up to a readership that we can only imagine. Such scenes show more than social satire or comic play. They offer more than fine-limned portraits of a schizophrenic or a sacred boy. They imagine a new way of reading, a way of dealing with the literary and the historical past as filtered through a fractured self:

It was quite an affecting sight, I used to think, to see him with the kite when it was up a great height in the air. What he had told me, in his room, about his belief in its disseminating the statements pasted on it, which were nothing but old leaves of abortive memorials, might have been a fancy with him sometimes. But not when he was out, looking up at the kite in the sky, and feeling it pull and tug at his hand. He never looked so serene as he did then. I used to fancy, as I sat by him of an evening, on a green slope, and saw him watch the kite high in the quiet air, that it lifted his mind out of its confusion, and bore it (such was my boyish thought) into the skies.

Compare this outdoor episode with the far more familiar, comforting occasion of the boy recalling his own times in his late father's library. There, great novels come out, "a glorious host, to keep me company":

They kept alive my fancy, and my hope of something beyond that place and time... It is curious to me how I could ever have consoled myself under my small troubles... by impersonating my favourite characters in them... When I think of it, the picture always rises in my mind, of a summer evening, the boys at play in the churchyard, and I sitting on my bed, reading as if for life.

The boy's imagination—impersonating fictive characters and finding consolation, fancy, and life in the act of reading—comes back, now transmuted in the scene of watching Mr. Dick. Instead of placing such sublimity within the room, they go outside. There is a physicality to Mr. Dick's airborne textualism; his writings pull and tug on him. A picture rises in the mind of the remembering narrator; a kite rises and lifts Mr. Dick's mind to the skies.

These are scenes of imaginative power, of the hold that textual engagement has on reader, writer, and observer. Both provoke an emotional response in David; both chronicle a moment of "affecting." Indeed, it is that very word *affecting* on which the idea of literary response hinges. The word emerged, in this adjectival form, in the eighteenth century specifically to connote the ways in which art, literature, or works of Nature could impress the mind and move emotions. Epic poetry, for example, in the words of Samuel Johnson, "relates some great event in the most affecting manner." Scenes are affecting, whether they are played on stage or watched in nature. "Beauty in distress," wrote Edmund Burke, "is the most affecting beauty."[16]

I can think of no more perfect depiction of beauty in distress than the one David watches: Mr. Dick, momentarily lifted from his confusion, elevated into air. It is, in Burke's sense, almost a textbook moment of sublimity, and to reread David's own reminiscence of his moment in the library against this open-air remembrance is to find the possibility of something deeply affecting not on the fields of nature but inside a nook.

Beauty in distress. David's thinking back on summer evenings while the other boys played is both a close remembrance and a close reading. But such remembrance is possible, here, precisely because there is so little to remember. A private library can hold just so many books. David recalls his father's "small collection." The list of texts is as canonical as any that a reader of his time could find: a short list of the best in eighteenth-century novels. David reads closely, not simply in the sense of holding books to hand and to eye, but in the more modern sense of "close reading." He attends to the growth of character, to scenes of drama and desire, to verbal texture and its impact on his comfort and his growth. David reads closely, and can live inside these books, precisely because they are a small, representative collection.

Franco Moretti has trouble with this kind of close reading. He sees it as belying the true nature of a literary tradition, of deluding us into thinking that the "novel" finds its form in but a few, exemplary documents:

> The trouble with close reading (in all of its incarnations from the new criticism to deconstruction) is that it necessarily depends on an extremely small canon. This may have become an unconscious and invisible premise by now, but it is an iron one nonetheless: you invest so much in individual texts only if you think that very few of them really matter.[17]

I agree completely with Moretti's observation, but I disagree with what he takes to be its literary or its social implication. You invest so much in individual texts only if you think that very few of them really matter. Every reader makes a private canon for him- or herself. The life is limned according to selection. David's own favorite books— much like those of his later literary heirs—exist to be invested in. Close reading makes the self. Tell me the story of your life and, if you are like me, you will give me less a saga than a syllabus.

In this process of narrowing the canon, the reader locates him- or herself in tradition. If we are to have our own canon of "affecting sights" they must be limited, and must consist of a few great memories. We build a kind of coterie of authors much as we build a coterie of friendships. Limitation fosters affect. The fact remains that, for most of us, very few books really do matter.

That is the point. What David does, and what Mr. Dick cannot do, is to define what small selection personally matters out of the vastness of the reading life. Mr. Dick's project is endless. David's will come to fruition. Mr. Dick lives in a world of incompleteness. Taken together, these two figures represent the difference between mere prose and the novel. Mr. Dick just keeps writing. David will, eventually, make litera-ture. As the critic Alexander Welsh had put it, "in this novel about the 'progress' of a writer, every writer but the hero—or his muse—writes wildly or hopelessly."[18]

It is that word "hopelessly" on which things hang, for David is a writer, and a reader, of hope: "my hope of something beyond that place and time." Hope changes us and changes others, and *David Copperfield* (like all of Dickens) makes a claim for literature as both a verbal form and as a social good. David is a novelist of the emotions, one who can transform raw experience into feeling and form. In retelling his life with Mr. Dick, he gives literary structure to the story. He bequeaths to Mr. Dick an emotive relationship to his work; he assumes, imagines, fancies what goes on in the man's mind. "It was quite an affecting sight." That phrase shows us what literature should be, as David turns the endless, iterative mass of Mr. Dick's life work into a story with an arc of drama and an ache of reminiscence. And when we watch, with David, the kite lose its lift and flutter, we see Mr. Dick's interiority through David's eyes: "*he seemed* to wake gradually out of a dream; and *I remember to have seen* him take it up, and look about him in a lost way, *as if* they had both come down together, so that *I pitied him* with all my heart" (216, emphases mine). We may be watching Mr. Dick, but we are feeling with David. This is a world of what appears to be, of seeming and remembering, of "as if" giving us a pity in the heart. This is one of the signal moments in the novel when David himself becomes the novelist of the imagination. If he is born again at Betsey Trotwood's, he is born a writer. And here, the page on which he sets his eyes is not the writing sheet before him, but the rejected written leaves of Mr. Dick's Memorial, high on a string's end.

Mr. Dick imagines for us an alternative kind of literacy, a different relationship to the literary tradition that is neither salvific nor redemptive nor heroic but is, instead, endlessly self-therapeutic. Stanley Tick argued that he points "in the direction of the novelist as self-therapist," but Mr. Dick points to the reader as self-therapist, as well.[19] As readers, teachers, and critics, we should turn not to David in the library for affirmations of our affect, but instead, get out into the air. I return, once again, to Nicholas Dames's phrasing: we should not, I believe, privilege the "barrier that books can build between a vulnerable self and the hostile world." We should see books as enabling the life lived in that world, of relishing the vulnerability of the self, of letting ourselves be affected by the beauty that we see in our distress. The professor may imagine him- or herself in the world of David's childhood. But most of our jobs are more like Mr. Dick's, struggling with unfinishable manuscripts, working through a range of deep hurts to make sense of narrative and symbol, hoping for a professional apotheosis that, in the end, often leaves us less sited in the stars than at the whims of winds.

We spend our lives trying to make our own intentions known. But our readers misinterpret, students come away with half-formed understandings, and reviewers want the book that they would write instead of what we wrote. Mr. Dick is no different. He is a cipher to all but Betsey Trotwood. While others think him mad, she finds him truly sane. "Nobody knows," she asserts, "what that man's mind is, except myself" (204). And so, great reader of this textual enigma, she explains:

> 'Did he say anything to you about King Charles the First, child?'
> 'Yes, aunt.'
> 'Ah!' said my aunt, rubbing her nose as if she were a little vexed. 'That's his allegorical way of expressing it. He connects his illness with great disturbance and agitation, naturally, and that's the figure, or the simile, or whatever it's called, which he chooses to use.'

Aunt Betsey presages critical close reading. She and David form a classroom of two, a cottage-style tutorial in literary understanding. That which you do not understand, that which does not make sense as literal or mimetic expression (she explains) must be taken allegorically. Mr. Dick's writing lives in not in the world of things but in the world of figure and of simile. His inner disturbance finds expression in verbal trope. He is a writer and a reader, but he now becomes a character to be read.

Armed with her tutelage, David can read his newfound friend. When they fly the kite, and David sees the older man now in a state of joy and peace, it is his critical interpretation that we read. *He seemed, I see, as if, I pitied*. These are, as I had just suggested, phrases that make David into a creative writer, choosing, comparing, and feeling for his character. But they are phrases, too, that make him a creative reader, conscious of his own interpretation as he sees the world.

II.

These moves in *David Copperfield* provided generations of writers and readers, teachers and editors, with the templates for understanding literature and its traditions. The tensions between selection and comprehensiveness, between brevity and inclusion, between something linear and self-contained and something endless and sprawling—all of these tensions in the novel play themselves out in a literary history of modern reading.

But we can only take that history piecemeal. Each one of us selects a group of books, a clutch of memories, a set of observations and finds ourselves (as Aunt Betsey would say) in their allegories, or their figures, or their similes, or whatever it's called. The history of shaping literary tradition and our place in it remains a history of trying to figure out whatever it's called.

This is what much of nineteenth-century literary culture sought to do.[20] These days, it is unfashionable to make lists of great books, to shape syllabi of study along lines of judgment, to read closely in a few works valued for their form, their content, or their social impact. For the Victorians, however, books shaped the forms of value. In someone such as Frederic William Farrar (1831–1905) we see the blend of literary judgment and moral piety characteristic of one strand of the age: "The best books of man will throw more and more widely open . . . the Books of God." In August Comte's *Positivist Library* of 1851 we see something more general: "a collection of works of permanent value for habitual use." And in John Lubbock's "hundred best books" of 1886, we find a mix of moral uplift and personal affect: "I have picked out the books most frequently mentioned with approval by those who have referred . . . to the pleasure of reading."

Such idioms and ideologies informed the nineteenth-century's anthologistic energies. The social practice of excerpting, judging, and using fostered a reading climate in which novels of the nineteenth-century could give voice to small canons of appreciation.[21] The great collections of the mid-nineteenth century presented themselves as assemblies of beauties, as treasuries of reading. The very process of anthologizing worked to codify a small collection, not just of authors, but of extracts. From Francis Palgrave's *Golden Treasury of English Songs and Lyrics* of 1861 to Arthur Quiller-Couch's *Oxford Book of English Verse* of 1900, a set of aesthetic and ideological criteria governed selections. "Omissions," as Palgrave averred, are not due to "oversight." Instead, the volume as a whole contributes to a definition, in this case, of lyric verse as clear in expression, rich in feeling, unified in form, and true to life.[22] The "best" seems, by these measures, simply obvious. As Quiller-Couch had put it, in the Preface to his *Oxford Book*, "the best is the best." But what remains, for the anthologist, the critic, or the reader, is not just the judgment of others but the experience of the self. "To be sure, a man must come to such a task as mine haunted by his youth and the favourites he loved in days when he had much enthusiasm but little reading."[23]

My father had a library of such anthologies. A high-school teacher in the 1950s, he had assembled a small collection of books ready-made for the classroom and the cocktail party. An updated Palgrave was there, as were the American versions of such treasuries: collections edited by Louis Untermeyer and Maynard Mack. Most afternoons, I'd root around in these collections. My favorite, and the one I kept, was F. O. Matthiessen's *Oxford Book of American Verse* of 1950. I loved it not so much for what it held—page after page of nineteenth-century stanzas that I could barely grasp—but for how it held them: the positive, assured, and confident tone of Matthiessen's preface, bound in the authoritative deep blue of the unmistakably Oxford covers. "Fewer poets, with more space for each."[24] Such was his "first principle," as he called it, and it soon became mine. I set out to make my own personal selection from this book, and as I read and reread I came back to Matthiessen's preface: "We have lacked until very lately a formed critical tradition in anything like the European sense. But we have produced by now a body of poetry of absorbing quality." To read in this anthology was, thus, to be absorbed by it—not just attracted but soaked up, sponged in between its covers like a spill. As I look back on my formative afternoons, I think now of Leah Price's understanding of Dickens's own claims for "absorptive reading." That was the Copperfield experience; that was the experience of Quiller-Couch, haunted by the readings of his youth.

As I page through it now, I see this as a book of readings and reminiscences, of American poets "reading as if for life" and going back to the great classics for their inspiration. The first page has Anne Bradstreet beginning: "To Sing of Wars, of Captains, and of Kings, / of

Cities founded, Common-wealths begun, / For my mean pen are too superior things." The book begins with classic invocation, with a memory of Virgil's *Aeneid*: "Arma virumque cano," as any student of the 1950s would recall. In the final poem of the volume, Robert Lowell's "Falling Asleep over the *Aeneid*," Matthiessen's principles come full circle. Here, an old man in Concord, Massachusetts, dreams over his book, imagining himself as one of Virgil's warriors, but also remembering his own childhood. Concord is now a place of reading; not the site of war and action, as in Emerson's "Concord Hymn" (printed in this anthology) but a locale of leisure. The light is not upon the landscape but the book: in Lowell's opening line, "The sun is blue and scarlet on my page." And at its close, as the church bell rouses him, he wakes, and recalls:

> Mother's great aunt, who died when I was eight,
> Stands by the parlor sabre. 'Boy, it's late.
> Virgil must keep the Sabbath.' Forty years!
> It all comes back.

It all comes back. David Copperfield has become not just an "origin myth for literary scholars." He has become the template for anthologists and poets. His dead father's library becomes a personal collection, and his memory looks back to classic texts against which he will measure his own life. Matthiessen saw his own volume as containing poetry revealing "violent contrasts and unresolved conflicts," and in that revelation corresponding "thereby to American life." America, in his collection, is a new Rome, all its writers are potential Virgils. But this book shows, too, that there is no single *Aeneid* for everyone, no sole epic that defines the American people. Instead, it reveals that the best way to understand America is as an anthology itself, a collection of different voices, visions, and Virgilians.

III.

I think that Salman Rushdie has had similar experiences. His literary India is also a nation of contrasts and conflicts, and his *Midnight's Children* offers an anthology of voices reaching back to classic forms. If any novel of my time so fully and creatively confronts and transforms the Copperfield experience, it is this one. The lines of influence seem

clear: two stories of a boy born on a Friday's midnight; two tales
of young men coming to the writing life; two sprawling canvases of
nation, narrative, and knowledge, caging a menagerie of characters
and generations. Rushdie recalled, in a lecture of the 1990s, that
Dickens struck him as a "quintessentially Indian novelist," with his
juxtapositions of rich and poor, bureaucracy and personality, social
realism and fantastic imagination:

> In my earlier novels I tried to draw on the genius of Dickens.
> I was particularly taken with what struck me as his real innovation:
> namely, his unique combination of naturalistic backgrounds
> and surreal foregrounds. In Dickens, the details of place and
> social mores are skewered by a pitiless realism, a naturalistic
> exactitude that has never been bettered. Upon this realistic canvas
> he places his outsize character, in whom we have no choice
> but to believe because we cannot fail to believe in the world they
> live in. So I tried, in my novel *Midnight's Children*, to set against a
> scrupulously observed social and historical background...my
> 'unrealist' notion of children born at the midnight moment of
> India's independence, and endowed with magical powers by the
> coincidence...[25]

Rushdie's offers a sensitive, intuitive account of Dickens's own relationship to the novelistic past (his "innovation") together with his
influence on a young, Indian novelist. To find India in Dickens is no
less strange than to find Kafka, or Joyce, or the Internet, or postmod-
ernism. In Mr. Dick we see the outsize character set in a landscape of
naturalistic exactitude. In David Copperfield we see a child shaped by
pitiless social realities thrust into surreal foregrounds.

In Saleem Sinai, the hero/narrator of *Midnight's Children*, we see,
from the start, the tensions between these two models of self-writing
and self-reading:[26]

> I was born in the city of Bombay...once upon a time. No, that
> won't do, there's no getting away from the date: I was born in
> Doctor Narlikar's Nursing Home on August 15th, 1947. And
> the time? The time matters, too. Well then: at night. No, it's
> important to be more...On the stroke of midnight, as a matter
> of fact. Clock-hands joined palms in respectful greeting as

I came. Oh, spell it out, spell it out: at the precise instant of
India's arrival at independence, I tumbled forth into the world.
There were gasps. And, outside the window, fireworks and
crowds. A few seconds later, my father broke his big toe; but his
accident was a mere trifle when set beside what had befallen me
in that benighted moment, because thanks to the occult tyran-
nies of those blandly saluting clocks I had been mysteriously
handcuffed to history, my destinies indissolubly chained to those
of my country. For the next three decades, there was to be no
escape. Soothsayers had prophesied me, newspapers celebrated
my arrival, politicos ratified my authenticity. I was left entirely
without a say in the matter. I, Saleem Sinai, later variously
called Snotnose, Stainface, Baldy, Sniffer, Buddha and even
Piece-of-the-Moon, had become heavily embroiled in Fate—at
the best of times a dangerous sort of involvement. And I couldn't
even wipe my own nose at the time.[27]

This dazzling paragraph recasts the opening of *David Copperfield*, turning Dickens's realism into post-colonial magic. Rushdie fragments the
straightforward, Dickensian sentences. The boy's birth marks the
clock strike, just as David's does, but here the baby's cry seems to get
lost in the cries and fireworks of the new nation. *Spell it out, spell it out.*
Rushdie takes the self-narrating impulse of a Dickens hero and turns
it into immediate interpretation. We have no need of Betsey Trotwood's
tuition here; Saleem is, from his birth, a sign, a figure, a simile, an
allegory. Renamed according to his nose rather than his ancestry, he
lives in that Dickensian best-of-times/worst-of-times paradox.

If there is dazzlement in this first paragraph, it is the dazzlement
of *copia*. Dickens begins with simple sentences, Rushdie with mad verbiage. Like Mr. Dick, imprisoned by his own prolixity, Saleem can't seem
to write down anything without returning to a past, without an endlessly
recursive history behind his story. Like his Dickensian forebears, Saleem
is a creature of the page—though here, it is not just the page of writing
but "the perforated sheet," the soon-to-be marked whiteness that stands
between him and his remembered past. If there is an allegory of anything here, it is an allegory of reading and writing.

"I must commence," Saleem states, in a most Dickensian-sounding
set of phrases, "the business of remaking my life from the point at

which it really began" (4). And so, he tells the story of his grandfather Aadam Aziz, a German-trained physician who comes back to India, and who in 1915 has, by a convoluted set of consequences, been called to attend to the daughter of a local worthy. The young girl, beset by a raft of maladies, can only be examined through a perforated sheet: large cloth held before her, with a small hole cut into it. The girl's attendants have the job of holding the sheet up, moving the hole to the part of her body that requires the doctor's ministrations. At first, there is a pain in the stomach; then, on subsequent visits, a lump in the breast, a strain in the leg, and finally a longed-for and anticipated headache. Only then can Dr. Aziz see the young girl's face. And yet, to that point, he has examined her in every body part, dismembered, as it were, viewed and felt only through a hole in a bed sheet. He, and we, never see the full woman until the very end—until he proposes marriage.

It is a brilliant allegory. We read as through a perforated sheet, taking the bits and pieces of our observation and creating wholeness through it. Memory, too, is such a sheet: moments of clarity viewed through the scrim of time. Eventually, too, Dr. Aziz and his bride consummate their marriage on that sheet, and three small drops of blood appear, markers of love and of the body to be understood.

Dickens's page becomes Rushdie's sheet, the white space against which the marks of life are made. But Saleem is no David Copperfield. He cannot seem to choose or select what he needs to say. Everything spills forth from his pen. His servant Padma, gloriously and self-knowingly illiterate, cannot grasp why he writes so much. "But what is so precious," she asks, "to need all this writing-shiting?" (24). She may be unable to read or write, but she is a great cook, stirring the pots of boiling pickles and chutneys in the factory where Saleem is a tester. "So," she implores, "if you are going to spend all your time wrecking your eyes with that scribbling, at least you must read it to me." But Saleem keeps writing, there in the chutney factory. "Rising from my pages comes the unmistakable whiff of chutney" (43). That word, "rising," conjures the memory of other things that rose in David Copperfield: the picture "rising" in the boy's mind of his memory of reading, Mr. Dick's kite rising with its scribbles in the sky. What rises now is smell, as if the Dickensian page had been steeped in the spice of India. If he is to be what Rushdie called "a quintessentially Indian novelist," his pages, too, must smell like home.

And as we read, those pages smell more and more like poor Mr. Dick's. He had his Betsey Trotwood, ready to understand his mind, ready to allegorize his life into meaning. Saleem has Padma, literalist of the imagination, "bullying me back into the world of linear narrative, the universe of what-happened-next." "At this rate," she complains, "you'll be two hundred years old before you manage to tell about your birth" (44). So, too, we might say much the same about Mr. Dick and his Memorial. "History pours from my fissured body," says Saleem (45). So, too, it pours from Mr. Dick's.

Midnight's Children plays out the two ways of confronting the personal and literary past in *David Copperfield*. We watch its narrator struggle with multitudes of memories; we see him try, but fail, to select and arrange. He struggles in the universe of what-happened-next—a universe which Dickens, and the emerging writer David, will master. Rushdie himself prepares us for these readings. For in his magical-realist effusion, Dickens's phrases show up like (as he would say in his lecture) bits of reality on a surreal canvas. I was born; rising; midnight; the clock; the cry. David Copperfield, as much as Saleem Sinai, is "handcuffed to history." But his history proceeds in a linear way. He makes his life a memory of what happened next. Saleem, like his forbear Mr. Dick, can only spew the pages.

These are the paradoxes and the challenges of the Copperfield experience. In one sense, we want to find ourselves in books, to read as if for life, and to see literature as fostering, redemptive, and affirming. But, in another sense, we recognize that our own collection of memories is an anthology itself. We select from the things we lived and make a canon of remembrance. The Copperfield experience of the literary tradition teaches not just what to read but what to recall: selecting, ordering, and putting both books and memories together into a self. Is such a self, then, really true? Or is it shaped? What comes out of the end of this experience may be a hero who lives largely on the page: mediated, created, even a little unreliable, a character.

To think about reading and remembering in this way is to be affected and absorbed—not into complacency but into a delightful insecurity. Perhaps the only way to get out of the snare is to get rid of books and memories themselves. Or at the very least, to police them into a truce.

IV.

This is the provocation of Ray Bradbury's *Fahrenheit 451*, a story of a future without the book, a future lived along the level field of institutional control.[28] My contemporaries came to this book as the lament for political power over reading, as the best argument for reading as if for life. I came to it, though, almost by mistake.

My freshman year, I did little else but go to movies. My small, New England liberal arts college was famous for its film series, and we would leave our backpacks and troop into the great dining hall for evening after evening of Erich Rohmer, Rainer Maria Fassbinder, and Frederico Fellini. One week, it was Francois Truffaut, and by Friday, after *Jules and Jim* and *The 400 Blows*, we watched *Fahrenheit 451*. There, the fireman Montag (played by the chillingly affectless Oskar Werner) set out to burn the books and cope with his increasingly distant wife. The black-and-white future it painted seemed, for students of the 1970s, all too familiar (this was, on college campuses, the great age of architectural brutalism). But when Montag sat down at night and pulled the book out of his hiding place, some of us gasped. There was the first page of *David Copperfield* (the book many of us were reading in our literary surveys), its print come alive along the reader's finger. "Chapter One: I am Born." Werner read hesitantly, slowly, as if he were reading almost for the first time, and I thought, I must go back and read Bradbury's own story—a book about a world without books, a story I would read about people who had forgotten how to read.

Imagine my disappointment. There is no episode in Bradbury's *Fahrenheit 451* that corresponds to this scene in Truffaut's film. The novel seemed to me far more complex, less linear, more oblique than the movie version, which had ironed out the wrinkles in the plot to make a more straightforward science fiction allegory (I later read an interview in which Truffaut admitted that he set out to make the film without ever having read the book). Montag never picks up *David Copperfield* in the novel. Instead, he caches many books away, and when he visits the old teacher, Faber, he brings with him nothing less than the King James Bible.

Bradbury's novel is no simple allegory but an ambiguous account of books and power politics. At the heart of the story is the rationale for why there are no books left and why the remaining ones must be destroyed. The literary history it recounts is one of constant accretion. Books upon books came to be written, each for a different kind of reader, each for a different group. Everyone wanted their own experience to be recorded in a book, and soon, there were so many, and so many different and discordant ones, that there could be no unity of social life. As Beatty, the captain of the fire brigade, explains to Montag:

> With school turning out more runners, jumpers, racers, tinkerers, grabbers, snatchers, fliers, and swimmers instead of examiners, critics, knowers, and imaginative creators, the word "intellectual," of course, became the swear word it deserved to be. You always dread the unfamiliar. Surely you remember the boy in your own school class who was exceptionally "bright," did most of the reciting and answering while the others sat like so many leaden idols, hating him. And wasn't it this bright boy you selected for beatings and tortures after hours? Of course it was. We must all be alike. Not everyone born free and equal, as the Constitution says, but everyone *made* equal. Each man the image of every other; then all are happy, for there are no mountains to make them cower, to judge themselves against. So! A book is a loaded gun in the house next door. Burn it. Take the shot from the weapon. Breach man's mind. Who knows who might be the target of the well-read man? Me? I won't stomach them for a minute. And so when houses were finally fireproofed completely, all over the world...there was no longer need of firemen for the old purposes. They were given the new job, as custodians of our peace of mind, the focus of our understandable and rightful dread of being inferior; official censors, judges, and executors. That's you, Montag, and that's me. (55)

Bradbury published these lines in 1953, at the height of McCarthyism, at the close of decades of Stalinist purges, at the onset of what would become the complacent age of Eisenhower. When I read this speech twenty years later, I thought it overdone. Hadn't we gone beyond book burning; hadn't our liberal educations prepared us not for jumping and grabbing but for knowing and imagining; books were loaded guns, but weren't they better than the real guns that we watched, discharging in Asian fields each night on television?

Now, over forty years later, I think we have not come so far. Our classrooms have instrumentalized our education, and an increasing fear of difference has, again, made "intellectual" a swear word. I was one of those bright boys in school, and I still remember all the leaden idols in the seats around me, all the tauntings after hours. I thought, like David Copperfield, I would find solace in the book. Like Montag in the movie, I hoped to become reborn through reading.

Mine is a book for readers everywhere, but I am an American. Franco Moretti, in his critique of close reading, averred: "America is a country of close readers." And so it is. Not only in its traditions of academic New Criticism or deconstruction, but in its canons of the commonplace, America demands a close attention to the word. Mine is a country built on documents. Montag's boss reads his Constitution as we might read ours: fine-tuning the texture of language and intention. "Not everyone born free and equal, as the Constitution says, but everyone made equal." Curious for a fireman to be such an imaginative close reader. Beatty becomes a teacher for the new illiteracy, not simply writing books out of society, but carefully, almost syllogistically, arguing them out of existence. His is a careful, historical narrative. Montag sits silently, as much a student to his history as David Copperfield had sat with Betsey Trotwood, listening to her interpretation of her Mr. Dick. And much like Aunt Betsey, Beatty offers a singular insight into the self. "Nobody knows what that man's mind is except myself," she said. Beatty concludes, "That's you, Montag, and that's me." These both are episodes of affirmation, letting the student figure know just how to read the world.

Saleem Sinai's initial tutor is the illiterate Padma, goading him to tell his story linearly, briefly, and effectively. Her wish for a "what happened next" tale is the wish of everyone who thinks that literature should have a straight-lined plot. It is the wish of the anthologist, who puts together poems, one after the other, to create a narrative of literary history. What happened next, we ask, as we turn pages of the Oxford books or the *Norton Anthology*.

The literary tradition is not so simple. It is less a tale of what happened next than a complex of fits and starts, of things begun and rediscovered. Literature is a large, sprawling, complex aggregation, full of things we probably will never read. It is not, of course, just made up of a few novels, plays, or poems, or a few writers privileged as the great. But that is the way we make sense of it, the way we give it meaning for ourselves in our lives. Bradbury's novel is far less dramatic than Truffaut's film, but it makes its point: books proliferate, and the job of the reader is to select and organize. That is a daunting task, requiring not skill in jumping or tinkering or flying, but knowing and critically assessing. In the absence of such skills, all you can do is just get rid of every book and leave it at that. Mr. Dick is fortunate in his fictive worlds: he can go on, endlessly writing; Saleem Sinai has his constraints, but when we start his novel we are made to think, along with Padma, will this ever end?

I've argued in this chapter that the literary past must be remade, selectively, by each of us. The meaning that we grant to literature comes through a process of selection. If we are to find ourselves in books, then it must be with a literature that can fit on a bookshelf.

Let me conclude with one more scene from Dickens, one with perhaps the closest and most self-referring reader in all of his fictions. *Great Expectations*, much like *David Copperfield*, opens with memories of parents' traces.[29] Having lost both mother and father before he could remember them, Pip must rely on mental pictures conjured from their tombstones. "The shape of the letters on my father's [tombstone] gave me an odd idea that he was a square, stout, dark man, with curly black hair." For his mother, her "character" lies in the "character and turn of the inscription." Young Pip is always looking for his past on such imaginative pages. So, too, is Joe Gargery, the sweet, barely literate, and henpecked husband of his guardian aunt. When Pip learns the rudiments of writing and reading, he shows Joe his first efforts, and the blacksmith "reads": "Why here's a J and an O equal to anythink. Here's a J and an O, Pip, and a J-O, Joe." As he continues:

> Give me a good book, or a good newspaper.... When you do come to a J and a O, and says you, 'Here, at last, is a J-O, Joe,' how interesting reading is!

Joe is the closest of close readers. He makes a personalized meaning out of letters, quite literally finding himself in everything he comes across. Unlike Mr. Dick, he offers up the most succinct of literate imaginations. A two-letter word is about as small as a word can be, and in its truncation, JO gives all that Joe needs to find. Mr. Dick only gives us part of Dickens, and the endlessness of his textual production stands in dramatic contrast to Joe's distillations.

Mr. Dick and Joe Gargery offer the two poles of reading. Though superficial simpletons, they call attention to the ways in which the textualized past becomes part of the person. They give us two extreme versions of the canon: for one, endless verbiage; for the other, just two letters. They offer us two inimitable models of literacy, the minimalist and the maximalist. Even when Joe eventually learns to write, by the novel's end, he remains unaltered. "There was," Pip reports, "no change whatever in Joe."

Is there a change in us? Does literacy make us different? Does the encounter with the literary past, our selection of personalized texts, our creation of a private canon—do these activities change us or only reaffirm whom we have always been? Each one of us will have a different answer. In the novels I have looked at here, each character has a distinct relationship to reading, writing, and the literary past. Some grow, some stagnate. In some sense we are all, like Saleem Sinai, handcuffed to history. We read in our local moment and our cultural condition. In the end, to read "as if for life" is not so much to read in order to keep living but to place ourselves in that world of "as if," to realize that in the fictions of the past lie provocations for our present. Joe Gargery, in some sense, comes alive in those lines where he finds a J and O. Mr. Dick is never livelier than when his lettered kites soar. To be the hero of your own life is not just to live it but to write it, read it, and set it on the bookshelf with all those bound "as if's" of literature.

Notes

1. Charles Dickens, *The Personal History of David Copperfield* [The Oxford Illustrated Dickens] (Oxford: Oxford University Press, 1989).
2. Nicholas Dames, "On Hegel, History, and Reading as if for Life," *Victorian Studies* 53 (2011): 437. See, too, D. A. Miller, *The Novel and the Police* (Berkeley and Los Angeles: University of California Press, 1988); Martha Nussbaum, *Love's Knowledge: Essays on Philosophy and Literature* (New York: Oxford University Press, 1990), 230–3; Philip Davis, *The Experience of Reading* (London: Routledge, 1992), xiv.
3. Dickens, *David Copperfield*, xii.

4. Louisa May Alcott, *Little Women, Little Men, Jo's Boys* (New York: Library of America, 2005), 46.

5. "The boy Henry soon became a desultory reader of every book he found readable, but these were commonly eighteenth-century historians because his father's library was full of them....So, too, he read shelves of eighteenth-century poetry..." Henry Adams, *The Education of Henry Adams* (Boston: Houghton Mifflin, 1918), 36.

6. Esther Forbes, *Johnny Tremain: A Novel for Old and Young* (Boston: Houghton Mifflin, 1943), 96: "Bound back copies of the *Observer, Paradise Lost, Robinson Crusoe... Tom Jones...* and now he remembered with gratitude how his mother had struggled to teach him so that this world might not have been forever closed to him. How she had made him read to her when he would have been playing...So he sat for hours in the Lornes' sunny parlor, the books about him stretching to the ceiling."

7. Ankhi Mukherjee, *What is a Classic? Postcolonial Writing and the Invention of the Canon* (Stanford: Stanford University Press, 2014), 1–3.

8. Edward Said, *Culture and Imperialism* (New York: Random House, 1993), 106.

9. Moretti has been developing the notion of "distant reading" since *The Way of the World: The Bildungsroman in European Culture* (London: Verso, 1987), through *Graphs, Maps, Trees: Abstract Models for Literary History* (London: Verso, 2007), and culminating in *Distant Reading* (London: Verso 2013).

10. Moretti, *Distant Reading*, 211.

11. See, for example, Mark Spilka, *Dickens and Kafka* (Bloomington: Indiana University Press, 1963); Jay Clayton, *Charles Dickens in Cyberspace: The Afterlife of the Nineteenth Century in Postmodern Culture* (Oxford: Oxford University Press, 2003); Barry McCrea, *In the Company of Strangers: Family and Narrative in Dickens, Conrad, Joyce, and Proust* (New York: Columbia University Press, 2011).

12. "There are odd parallels between the two times...the telegraph and the Internet; Babbage's Analytical Engine and the digital computer; nineteenth-century sound technology and virtual reality; Frankenstein's monster and genetic clones; automata and artificial-life research" (Clayton, *Charles Dickens in Cyberspace*, 8).

13. See Leah Price, *How to Do Things with Books in Victorian Britain* (Princeton: Princeton University Press, 2012), 72–106.

14. Stanley Tick, "The Memorializing of Mr. Dick," *Nineteenth-Century Fiction* 24 (1969): 142–53.

15. See Alexander Welsh, *From Copyright to Copperfield: The Identity of Dickens* (Cambridge, Mass.: Harvard University Press, 1987), 116–19.

16. *OED*, s.v., *affecting*.

17. Moretti, *Distant Reading*, 48. For engagements and critiques, see Joseph North, "What's 'New Critical' about 'Close Reading'? I. A. Richards and his New Critical Reception," *New Literary History* 44 (2013): 141–57; Natalia Cecire, "Ways of Not Reading Gertrude Stein," *ELH* 82 (2015): 281–312.

18. Welsh, *From Copyright to Copperfield*, 116.

19. Tick, "Memorializing," 150.

20. See W. B. Carnochan, "Where Did the Great Books Come From, Anyway?" *Stanford Humanities Review* 6:1 (1998): 51–64, and "Afterword: 'A Matter *Discutable*': The Rise

of the Novel," in the reprinting of Ian Watt, *The Rise of the Novel* (Berkeley and Los Angeles: University of California Press, 2001), 303–22.

21. See Leah Price, *The Anthology and the Rise of the Novel* (Cambridge: Cambridge University Press, 2000).

22. Francis Palgrave, *Palgrave's Golden Treasury of Songs and Lyrics*, Book Third, ed., J. H. Fowler (London: Macmillan, 1903), xi.

23. Arthur Quiller-Couch, *The Oxford Book of English Verse, 1250–1900* (Oxford: Clarendon Press, 1900), ix.

24. A few sentences in this and the following paragraph adapt and recast material from Seth Lerer, "Falling Asleep over the History of the Book," *PMLA* 212 (2006): 229–34. Quotations from Matthiessen's volume are from F. O. Matthiessen, ed., *The Oxford Book of American Verse* (Oxford: Oxford University Press, 1950).

25. Salman Rushdie, "Influence," in *Step Across This Line* (New York: Vintage, 2003), 71.

26. See Ankhi Mukherjee, "The Rushdie Canon," in Robert Eaglestone and Martin McQuilian, eds, *Salman Rushdie: Contemporary Critical Perspectives* (London: Bloomsbury, 2013), 9–21; Peter Morey, "Salman Rushdie and the English Tradition," in Abdulrazak Gurnah, ed., *The Cambridge Companion to Salman Rushdie* (Cambridge: Cambridge University Press, 2007), 29–43.

27. *Midnight's Children* (New York: Vintage, 2011), 3.

28. *Fahrenheit 451* (New York: Simon & Shuster, 2013).

29. See Max Byrd, "Reading in Great Expectations," *PMLA* 91 (1976): 259–65.

3

My *1984*

> It was a bright cold day in April, and the clocks were striking thirteen. Winston Smith, his chin nuzzled into his breast to escape the vile wind, slipped quickly through the glass doors of Victory Mansions, though not quickly enough to prevent a swirl of gritty dust from entering along with him. (CW IX: 3)[1]

Almost seventy years after its first publication, the opening of Orwell's *1984* still disorients us. No clocks in our time strike thirteen, and the entrance to the portentously named Victory Mansions rubs harshly against the vile wind and the gritty dust. As the most famous of modern dystopian fictions, *1984* presents a world, now, so familiar as to be almost cliché: a world of surveillance and suspicion, in which official words have only the most passing of resemblances to social realities, in which the past is constantly rewritten to conform to an elusive present. Within a year of the book's publication in 1949, the term "Orwellian" was already connoting the contradictions of a broken future, and by the 1960s, the Newspeak of *1984* joined with Orwell's polemical reflections in his "Politics and the English Language" to provide my generation with a magnifying lens for official deceit.[2] Those strange distillations of the novel—*unperson, thoughtcrime, doublethink*—resonated in our ears with the euphemisms of that essay: "rectification of frontiers," "elimination of unreliable elements." By the time Francis Ford Coppola's *Apocalypse Now* appeared in theaters in 1979, its military order, "terminate with extreme prejudice," could be accepted as commonplace of our Orwellian idiom. "Such phraseology is needed if one wants to name things without calling up mental pictures of them," Orwell avowed in "Politics and the English Language."

This is the language of what David Bromwich has called "revolutionary euphemism," where horror translates into phrases "colorless by design."[3] At the heart of political control is not only force but style. Language is the medium of politics, and manipulations of the literary past have always been a tool of social engineering. Orwell made us aware of (again in Bromwich's words) "the ease and invisibility of euphemism," and the past two decades have seen a compelling reassessment of his fiction, essays, and reflections.[4] As Edward Said put it, Orwell has become an "exemplary figure ... whose significance derives from but nevertheless seems to transcend the immediate force of [his] native context." Or, to put it with the bluntness of Christopher Hitchens, Orwell "still matters."[5]

My *1984* still matters, but less for its vision of a social future than its retrospective of a literary past. For all of its anticipation, it remains a novel of traditions: a mosaic of allusions to canonical authors, institutional practices, and personal tastes. It testifies to Orwell's history of reading, reaching back through school at Eton and through a lifetime in the book trade, journalism, and public authorship.[6] He had a deep (if, by scholarly standards, largely intuitive) understanding of literature and language as forms of history. At the time of his death in 1950, he possessed over five hundred books, and that was only a fraction of the number he had owned and read throughout his life.[7] He knew as much about the Latin of the past as he knew of the vernacular of the present.[8] How else could he claim, in "Bookshop Memories" of 1936, that he would "sooner give a child a copy of Petronius Arbiter than Peter Pan"?[9] He read Chaucer as well as Dante, and his essays fill themselves with comments on the Saints as much as on sinners. Since early childhood, Dickens was a constant literary companion (CW, XII: 28), and his writings of the 1930s and 40s reveal an acquaintance with virtually every writer in the English and American canon.

Orwell's *1984* stands as my vantage point for looking at the literary tradition in history. It offers a way of seeing literature as an ever-changing phenomenon, not as a bookshelf but a breakdown. The novel explores how tradition emerges as a category of the past: how notions of historical, social, and linguistic change developed to grant a chronological, linear movement to the canon and its contexts. Its episodes chart developments in reading and interpretation throughout literary history, from allegory to philology to fable, from Chaucer and Dante to C. S. Lewis and Kenneth Grahame. Reading Orwell (as one recent critic has put it) "is to be plunged into an active network or field of writing," where references take us to other references, where allusions concatenate into canons. Orwell "still matters" because he teaches us to read, and to read like Orwell is to develop "a feeling of interconnection" among the texts that overlap and layer in his prose.[10]

Orwell still matters because he has taught us, too, to write as well as read. He had a deep, abiding influence on how we have told and retold the literary past. The way he juxtaposes ideology and aesthetics, the way he limns the contours of a culture of surveillance, the way he sees the literary vernacular denatured into Newspeak—the way he does all these things profoundly influenced our way of looking at relationships of inwardness and power in the history of literature. Orwell has sensitized us to a way of seeing tradition as a mutable thing, constantly subject to revision and rewriting, something darker, perhaps, than we had once thought.

This chapter, therefore, has a double focus: one that explores Orwell's own engagements with the literary past and his reflections on the canon, and another that illustrates how those engagements have reshaped the ways in which we read and write about that canon. Orwell still matters not simply for his political prescience but for his literary vision. *1984* had taught that history can be rewritten; poetry is subject to re-editing; the past, as Winston recognized, can (must?) be "brought up to date." *1984* provokes our assessment of what we do *to* and *with* old texts. It makes us question our relationship to a tradition shaped by personal experience and institutional archive. Orwell becomes my guide not to what will be, but what has been.

I.

"It was a bright cold day in April." To start with April is to start in the literary spring of the earliest English poetry. Medieval poems that associated spring and love, April and desire, were legion. Lyrics such as "Betwene Mersh and Averil," "When the nightingale sings the woodes waxen grene," and "Lenten is come with love to toun," had long been mainstays of anthologies, and Orwell would have read them (and a host of others) in books he owned: Arthur Quiller-Couch's *Oxford Book of English Verse* (1923 edition), Thomas Percy's *Reliques of Ancient English Poetry* (1926 edition), and Chambers' and Sidgwick's *Early English Lyrics* (1921 edition). The call to April had long been a trope of opening, but it was no more famous than in Chaucer's first lines of the *Canterbury Tales*:

> Whan that Aprille with his shoures sote
> The droghte of Marche hath perced to the rote
> And bathed every veyne in swiche licour
> Of which vertu engendred is the flour;
> Whan Zephirus eek with this swete breeth
> Inspired hath in every holt and heeth
> The tendre croppes, and the yonge sonne
> Hath in the Ram his halve cours y-ronne...

Chaucer's is both a seasonal description and a literary invocation. It locates the poem in the new beginnings of the earth—in a period of both vegetable and spiritual renewal. Literary creation takes place during the time of Creation itself. Much as the "swete breeth" of Zephirus "inspired" the growth of new plants, so the poet, too, is inspired by his subject. Chaucer sets his poem's opening along the axes of the calendar, the zodiac, and the liturgy. It is April; the sign of the sun has run halfway through the sign of the Ram; and now it is time to exercise the sacrament of pilgrimage.

Orwell read Chaucer in the then-standard edition of W. W. Skeat (he owned the 1920 edition), and Skeat's notes would have alerted him to the literary history of this passage, its zodiacal import, and its social implications.[11] So too, for any reader of the *Canterbury Tales* in the first decades of the twentieth century, Skeat's edition would have provided rules for speaking and appreciating Chaucer's verse: "An attentive reader will thus catch the swing of the metre, and will be carried along almost mechanically" (xxiii). Orwell's own sentences seem, when read aloud, to scan—though less in regular heroic couplets than in the iambs of popular vernacular. *It was a bright cold day in April and the clocks were striking*...Such sonic effects play well in a story of poetry and politics, with its snatches of remembered music hall and bits of street song. So, too, they would chime against the rhythms of another April, that of T. S. Eliot's "Waste Land":

> April is the cruelest month, breeding
> Lilacs out of the dead land, mixing
> Memory and desire, stirring
> Dull roots with spring rain.[12]

The first lines of "The Waste Land" challenge April's beauty and renewal, much as they challenge, formally, the swing of Chaucer's meter. The season's rebirth here looks less like resurrection than a kind of necromancy. The dead come back to life. Amidst the specifics of time and pace, of flower and dirt, there are the two, broad concept words, *memory* and *desire*, that take us out of the landscape and into ourselves. And at the formal level, Eliot jars the reader out of easy metrical complacencies. Each of the first three lines ends with the progressive form of the verb, each enjambs to the next line, miming the action-in-process. The lines rhyme, if they rhyme at all, on an unstressed, grammatical ending, the *–ing* of the verbs, making them ring unsurely in the ear.

It is a commonplace of criticism to locate *1984* along these axes of Chaucer and Eliot.[13] But only recently have scholars found in this beginning something far more powerful than mere allusion. Orwell opens with anxiety, but also allegory. There is a sense of the religious institutions behind both Chaucer and Eliot, a sense of looking back to mystery as well as meter. William Hunt, in a remarkable scholarly excavation of the medieval aura of this opening, has argued that "veiled allusions in Orwell's first sentence lead us, subliminally, into the world of pilgrimage and martyrdom, damnation and salvation." Like the *Divine Comedy*, Hunt concludes after a lengthy review of its Dantean intertexts, "*Nineteen Eighty-Four* is about the enlightenment of its protagonist, a pilgrim seeking the truth about the cosmos he inhabits."[14]

Orwell had lived with Dante for years. Among the books he owned at the time of his death were three editions and translations: one, in Italian, published in Florence in 1827; a second, the translation of John D. Sinclair from 1948; and a third, a bilingual text of the *Paradiso* from 1943.[15] He returned to the *Comedy* in the last year of his life, as he crowed in a letter to Anthony Powell in mid 1949, as he was dying of tuberculosis: "I'm reading Dante!" (CW XX: 126). And as a close reader of Eliot, he would have found much in the essay "Dante" (reprinted in the *Selected Essays* of 1932) to guide his engagement not just with the *Divine Comedy*, but with the range of Dante's work itself:

> In the middle of the journey of our life I came to myself within
> a dark wood where the straight way was lost. Ah, how hard a

> thing it is to tell of that wood, savage and dark and dense, the
> thought of which renews my fear!

The editors, commentators, and critics that encrusted this famous
opening would have taught Orwell that it would be in vain to look for
the real Italian forest in which an historical Dante lost his way. This is
no living woodland but the *selva oscura*, the forest of obscurities that
beset all interpreters along the road of life. Winston Smith finds himself in a dark wood redolent of the *Inferno*, what William Hunt has
called the "mental universe" of Dante and Chaucer.

That mental universe would have revealed itself not only in the
journey of the pilgrim but the writings of the poet. Years before the
Divine Comedy took shape, Dante looked back over his youthful poetry
to reshape early lyrics into a great narrative of love and salvation. The
Vita Nuova was composed in 1295, and it became a mainstay of
Victorian and Edwardian English amorists in the popular and
frequently reprinted translation of Dante Gabriel Rossetti:

> In that part of the book of my memory before the which is little
> that can be read, there is a rubric, saying *Incipit Vita Nova*. Under
> such rubric I find written many things; and among them the
> words I propose to copy into this little book; if not all of them,
> then at least their substance.[16]

Dante imagines memory as a book. This in itself was no new metaphor. Classical and late antique writers had written of the book of
memory, and Shakespeare's *Hamlet*, three hundred years after
Dante, could still reflect on the challenge of his father's ghost:
"Remember thee! / Yea, from the table of my memory / I'll wipe
away all trivial fond records, / . . . And thy commandment all alone
shall live / Within the book and volume of my brain" (*Hamlet*,
I.v.97–103).

Winston, too, has a book and volume to his brain. He surrepti-
tiously purchases a notebook and an old-style ink pen. He relishes the
creamy gloss of the paper and the flow of the ink. "To mark the paper
was the decisive act," and he begins by writing the date at the top of
the first page, "April 4, 1984." Part of Winston's anxiety, of course, lies
in being discovered with his diary. But part of his unsureness lies in the
date itself. Was it really April 4? Or for that matter, was it really 1984?

In a world in which clocks strike thirteen, what does it mean to mark the time and fix a date?

Winston's is a modern but it is, too, a medieval act. He opens up the book of memory and tries to transcribe its occluded lines. But everything is now unsure. Language has become decoupled from reality. There is a new vernacular in England, Newspeak, which cannot contain the nuances of old feelings. In such a world, what does it mean to try to write a diary, to recall a life lived on paper?

The opening of *1984* looks back on all of these tropes and traditions of the literary life. It asks us what it means to find ourselves in time and place, what the relationship may be between the word and the world, the writing and the self. These may be Chaucerian or Dantean moments, but they also are profoundly Dickensian ones, as well. What makes *1984* a novel, rather than merely fantasy or polemic or allegory, is precisely its literary self-consciousness, its opening with a Chaucerian April *and* a Dickensian chiming of the clock: "I was born...on a Friday,...the clock began to strike, and I began to cry, simultaneously." Orwell remarked, in an essay on Dickens of 1940, that he had first read *David Copperfield* when he was nine, and what he called "the mental atmosphere of the opening chapters was...immediately intelligible to me." Even as an adult, rereading the novel, "these passages lose nothing" (CW, XII: 28).

If they lost nothing, what did they gain the Orwell of *1984*? David begins his life on a Friday, and in some sense, so does Winston Smith. We know that Orwell originally planned to have the book begin on Good Friday. The date in his first draft of the novel, April 4, 1980, would have been Good Friday; and April 4, 1947 (the year in which he began writing) was the sacred day as well. Friday, too, was a day of portent for the *Canterbury Tales*: the Nun's Priest tells his story of contesting barnyard animals in mock Fall ("and on a Friday fell all this meschaunce"), and scholars had long known that, if you read the opening astrology aright, you find the pilgrims arriving at Canterbury on a Friday (the one date that Chaucer evokes in the poem, April 18, hovers around the dates of Good Friday for 1389 and 1394).[17]

Orwell re-allegorizes Dickens through Dante and Chaucer. He transforms the techniques and temper of the realist novel of personal growth into the futurist story of personal decline. Each scene of writing calls up a new memory; each scene of textual destruction questions the validity of memory itself. As Winston traces letters in his diary, we see him not so much writing as un-writing his past. What he wants to transcribe falls victim to new memories. Though trying to put down a linear succession of events—what happened next—he falls into a reverie of what had happened on the job. And what had happened was the Two Minutes Hate, the release of anger against the traitorous Emmanuel Goldstein, the one who broke with Big Brother in the founding of the new order. The point about Goldstein is not simply physical appearance (clearly a caricature of Leon Trotsky), or even his heresy, but his authorship.[18] For Goldstein's sin is writing:

> There were also whispered stories of a terrible book, a compen-
> dium of all the heresies of which Goldstein was the author and
> which circulated clandestinely here and there. It was a book with-
> out a title. People referred to it, if at all, simply as *The Book*. But one
> knew of such things only through vague rumours. (CW IX: 15–16)

What would the title be of Winston's book of heresies? Would it be found in that first date, in his name, or in something of the literary past that Orwell obliquely evokes? Winston's, much like Dante's, might be considered a book of the new life, an assembly of past texts rewritten for a new present.

More than a collocation of remembrances or tropes, these first moves of *1984* challenge the very notion of a literary tradition. In the world of Big Brother, the ultimate crime is one of literary agency itself. Words multiply on Winston's creamy page. Goldstein's book brings together all his authored heresies. But here, on Airstrip One in Oceania, there is no writing, only rewriting. Past documents must be recast in line with present political realities. A prediction of economic productivity needs to be rewritten to bring it into line with just what was produced; a claim about a military campaign must be reshaped to appear to have predicted the outcome of that campaign. Winston's work in the Ministry of Truth is the work of paper. Terse Newspeak instructions come to him on rolled slips. He recalls back issues of *The Times*, rewrites the stories as instructed, and then sends the slips down the "memory hole" for destruction:

> As soon as all the corrections which happened to be necessary
> in any particular number of *The Times* had been assembled and

collated, that number would be reprinted, the original copy destroyed, and the corrected copy placed on the files in its stead. This process of continuous alteration was applied not only to newspapers, but to books, periodicals, pamphlets, posters, leaflets, films, sound-tracks, cartoons, photographs—to every kind of literature or documentation which might conceivably hold any political or ideological significance. Day by day and almost minute by minute the past was brought up to date. (CW IX: 42)

Textuality is no guarantee of truth here; documentation loses its historical validity and lives permanently in the present. And, as Winston will learn, all the keepers of the word will find themselves corrected.

II.

And a few cubicles away, a mild, ineffectual, dreamy creature named Ampleforth, with very hairy ears and a surprising talent for juggling with rhymes and metres, was engaged in producing garbled versions—definitive texts, they were called—of poems which had become ideologically offensive, but which for one reason or another were to be retained in the anthologies. (CW IX: 44–5)

Orwell was fascinated by editions.[19] Throughout his essays, he attends not only to the content but the form of books: to cheap editions, paperbacks, Everymans, and firsts. He knew that literary history was a history of editing, and often editing away, things deemed offensive by a later time. In his essay on Dickens, Orwell recollects how the book called *The Fairchild Family* was once "a standard book for children," but in his time, its doctrine of "breaking the child" had come to seem too harsh. "This evil book is now issued in pretty-pretty expurgated editions, but it is well worth reading in the original version" (CW XII: 29). Such expurgation had long been a mainstay of the editorial world, and this moment in *1984* speaks to the arc of reading and rewriting not just in the past but in our own time.

Long before print fixed words in type, scribes copied poetry and prose into new compilations for new readers. From his copy of Skeat's *Works of Geoffrey Chaucer*, Orwell would have known of variants and errors, of editors who had relied on "inaccurate texts," of habits of recasting Chaucer's verse to fit more modern expectations of prosody. Often, as Skeat noted, "the restoration of the true reading shocks the reader's sense of propriety." But an "attentive reader," we recall, "will catch the swing of the metre."

1984 offers a tale of what it means to become an attentive reader, and its fascinations with re-editing and rewriting resonate with discussions Orwell would have found in his own library. The verse of the sixteenth century, for example, had long tested editors. Differences between poems in manuscript and early print raised questions about the intention of a writer, or the state of the language, or the relationships between past idiom and present taste. Norman Ault, in his anthology, *Elizabethan Lyrics* (whose 1925 edition Orwell owned), made clear his desire to edit poems from the oldest manuscripts.[20] Some of his texts had previously escaped "the vigilance of editors." Other texts had been so fastidiously presented in the past, that their musicality and lilt had been lost by experts "who seem to me to sacrifice aesthetic to antiquarian and philological considerations." But, Ault concludes his Introduction, no edition is perfect: "misprints and other mistakes abound," and no manuscript or early printed book could be supposed to be a "fair copy."

For all his interest in the past and for all his fascination with the language, Orwell was no antiquarian or philologist. But he clearly absorbed from his editions a sense of what it had meant to put together a "definitive text" or to assemble an anthology. To read *1984*, however, with such antiquarian or philological sensibilities—as I do—is to see how much of its action centers on copying, transcribing, rewriting, and destroying texts. I have a copy of Ault's volume beside me, with its claim to have offered "for the first time a wholly intelligible and complete text" of some of its poems. And then I open *1984* and find, in its appendix on Newspeak, the claim that "in the future," old works of history and literature "would be unintelligible." To read that "pre-revolution literature could only be subjected to ideological translation" is to direct me to my own bookshelf, to remember the story of such translations in the past (CW IX: 428).

Ault misses what Orwell prepared us now to see: that early printed books were both the ammunition and the target of a war of ideologies. Our current sense of the Renaissance English past is filtered through the Orwellian, and its most important modern scholars grew up under his shadow. Take, for example, the Tudor historian G. R. Elton.[21] Born Gottfried Ehrenburg in Germany and a Nazi-era émigré to England, Elton helped redefine the study of the age of Henry VIII as one of power and enforcement. In books such as *The Tudor Revolution in Government* (based on his 1948 University of London thesis and published in 1953) and *Policy and Police* (1972), Elton revealed a courtly culture lived less to the tune of "Green Sleeves" than to the sound of knocks on doorways in the middle of the night. Henry VIII's break with Rome led, in his view, to the establishment of a thought-machine designed to stamp out resistance to the new and to rewrite the old. This was a world run through command of texts, a world where old books were condemned, a world in which the very writing of the word "pope" was a crime. Books and manuscripts that had that word in them were seized by agents of King Henry (working under the instruction of his chief minister, Thomas Cromwell). It was a time, to appropriate Orwell's words, of "the position of the writer in an age of State control"; an age, in Elton's phrasing, when "any signs of resistance were stamped out by violence."[22] If we shudder at the fate of parents being turned in by their children in *1984*, we also shudder at the state of England in the late 1530s, where men and women were reported for "dangerous talk," and where "a relative, friend, acquaintance, or almost stranger" could hear something spoken, report verbal crime, and thus "discharge his duty" (*Policy and Police*, 331). This was, like Airstrip One, an England in which the operative verb was to "conceal," and that word shows up with as much striking frequency in the documents under Elton's archival purview as it does in *1984*.[23]

"Concealment" is everywhere, as, well, in Stephen Greenblatt's *Renaissance Self-Fashioning*, the field-defining study of my generation.[24] Greenblatt's work helped effect a shift in academic scholarship away from formal close readings of privileged literary texts and toward a broader historical awareness of how those texts participated in systems of power and control. Greenblatt's courtier and politician lived along the edge of "outward compliance and inward silence" (69). Politics was theater and theater was politics. And at the center of it stood the monarch and the instruments of information. Like Elton, Greenblatt set out to demystify what historians had long seen as a "lighthearted" and "charming" age of Henry VIII. In Greenblatt's arresting analogy, "conversation with the king himself must have been like small talk with Stalin" (136–7). Henry, in this account, routinely eliminated his cohorts, such that the "survival rate for those closest" to him "roughly resembles the actuarial record of the First Politburo" (15). And for Thomas More, caught between conscience and commitment, what kept him going for as long as he could was a "sense of human absurdity," a sense of "life lived at a perpetual remove from reality" (27).

It is precisely this split between perception and conviction that motivates the Inner Party faithful of *1984*, and it is precisely these analogies to mid-twentieth-century totalitarianism that compels us to see Orwell in the archive. In fact, Orwell had long fascinated Greenblatt, going back to his Yale undergraduate thesis, *Three Modern Satirists*, where Orwell formed part of a larger arc of mid-twentieth-century British social critique.[25] Granted, this is the work of a twenty-one-year-old, but in its summaries and judgments we can feel the fascinations with a world of surreption and desire that would characterize the idioms of *Renaissance Self-Fashioning*. Greenblatt recognized the relationships of language and feeling throughout Orwell's work, stressed the ways in which *1984* alters history "to suit the needs of the moment" (69), and called attention to the nature of civilization as dress and ornament. O'Brien, in Greenblatt's account, "relentlessly strips away man's protective clothing, the robes of civilization and culture, the garments of refinement, health, and common sense" (71). Compare this phrasing with the account, fifteen years later, in *Renaissance Self-Fashioning*, of Thomas More, living out a stage play of costume and stage-prop, recognizing that the rhetoric of public life is but a dress. When Greenblatt quotes More's version of a peasant's view of kingship—"He seems to me to be a man in an embroidered garment" (27)—or when he attends to passages in *Utopia* where a character appears "in a philosopher's attire" (35), he brings us back to Orwell's "robes of civilization." What is the "real self?" Greenblatt makes the world of Thomas More and Cromwell ask again and again, much as he found it asked of Winston Smith. And, after working through the undergraduate's attempts to understand Orwell's responses to the post-War Soviet state, we turn to *Renaissance Self-Fashioning* with knowing nods. "Revolution, as Marx understood, can have no traffic with inner intimations of unreality" (27).

I hear Orwell's voice behind statements such as this one: statements that juxtapose ideology and aesthetics, social performance and inner feeling. I hear his voice, too, in a range of current debates on the canon and its teaching. Should *Huckleberry Finn* live, uncut, in a local library? The question dogged the book from the moment of its publication. The Concord, Massachusetts, public library banned the book in 1885, deeming it (in the words of the report in the *Boston Transcript*) "rough, coarse, and inelegant, dealing with a series of experiences not elevating." Huck's own itching and scratching were deemed obscene by the New York Public Library in 1905.[26] Orwell had commented on how the book pushed the limits of decorum, reporting how Twain felt the word "Hell" would be "just what Huck would have said," but in the end agreeing with his wife that "the word could not possibly be printed."[27] But it was not until the 1980s and 90s that the novel's epithet for the runaway slave, Jim, provoked demands for its outright removal from curricula and canons. Some have gone so far to create new editions. "Publisher Tinkers with Twain," announced *The New York Times* on January 4, 2011, in response to an edition of the book put out by New South Books. *The Times* quotes the publisher: "We didn't undertake this lightly. If our publication fosters good discussion about how language affects learning and certainly the nature of censorship, then difficult as it is likely to be, it's a good thing."

Is any of this likely to be a good thing? Language certainly affects learning. There is, in this reporting, an Orwellian feel to the publisher's self-defense, a strange echo of the challenges of Newspeak and the life of doublethink. "Winston," a rewriter of the past, "was good at this kind of thing" (CW IX: 46). The ministers of *1984* would surely claim that their revisions were not undertaken lightly. To read the history of editing is to see layers of revision, to see what the medievalist in me would call a "palimpsest" of texts—old versions erased, new versions overwritten. And yet in the right light, you can see them all. Winston expressed it exactly in these terms. History, he noted, was a "palimpsest, scraped clean and re-inscribed exactly as often as was necessary." The word reveals a deep sense not just of the contents but the very physicality of textual transmission. His image locates history in the world of the pre-print, the world before paper, when texts could be inked and scraped on animal skin.[28] Chaucer had complained, famously, to his scribe Adam that his mistakes compelled him to rewrite his work: "So ofte adaye I mot thy werk renewe, / It to correcte and eke to rubbe and scrape." And Winston, sad scribe to his own self-dictation, revels in the physicality of his experience: the creaminess of the paper, the touch of the pen nib, the flow of the ink. He will become, throughout his own re-education, something of a palimpsest himself, scraped clean of old memories and re-inscribed exactly. As O'Brien will tell him after his arrest, "You will be lifted clean out from the stream of history."

What does it mean to lift a literary voice clean out from history? Poor Ampleforth himself is not immune to erasure. Towards *1984*'s close, as Winston languishes in prison, "the poet Ampleforth shambled into the cell." He'd been arrested for leaving the word "God" in the definitive edition of the poems of Kipling:

> "I could not help it!" he added almost indignantly, raising his face to look at Winston. "It was impossible to change the line. The rhyme was 'rod'. Do you realize that there are only twelve rhymes to 'rod' in the entire language? For days I had racked my brains. There WAS no other rhyme." (CW IX: 242–3)

Ampleforth continues: "Has it ever occurred to you that the whole history of English poetry has been determined by the fact that the English language lacks rhymes?"[29]

A fact of language has become the fate of poets. English never was as rich in rhymes as other European languages.[30] And yet, *1984* is full of rhymes. The verbal world of the proles echoes with the half-remembered stanzas of old verse: "Oranges and lemons, say the bells of St. Clement's." Mr. Charrington, the proprietor of the antique shop that will become Winston's hideaway, recalls it as "a rhyme we had when I was a little boy." The line echoes throughout the last third of the novel, as Winston hears it again and again and as he tries to reconstruct the rhymes of the stanza as it once was known: lemons/St. Clement's; farthings/St. Martin's; pay me/Old Bailey. It is not until his confrontation with O'Brien that the whole text of the poem appears. When Winston queries if he knew the old rhyme, O'Brien finishes the stanza: "When I grow rich, say the bells of Shoreditch." "You knew the last line!" Winston exclaims, and O'Brien simply responds, "Yes, I knew the last line."

Ampleforth may think he knows something about last lines, but long before his arrest he has already been prisoner to the lexicon. "There WAS no other rhyme." The history of literature—like the Party itself—teaches that there is always another rhyme, always another way of making books acceptable to audiences reared on ideology rather than idiom. Poor Ampleforth belies his name: no ample storehouse of potential words, he is trapped by the limitations of his knowledge.

III.

One lunchtime, early in the novel, Winston stands in line to get his pannikin of stew, and he turns around to find his friend. "Syme was a philologist, a specialist in Newspeak. Indeed he was one of the enormous team of experts now engaged in compiling the Eleventh Edition of the Newspeak Dictionary" (CW IX: 51). Philology was the science of words, and English literary and linguistic history, well into Orwell's time, was written by philologists. By the middle of the nineteenth century, philology had been elevated to "the science of sciences." By the century's end, the philologist himself—whether in the person of the Oxford professor Max Müller or the first editor of the *Oxford English Dictionary*, James A. H. Murray—had become the arbiter of cultural belonging. The "philological eminence" of these men, and their contemporaries and successors, gave voice to a view of language as a vehicle for cultural advancement, or decay.[31] By the 1940s, at least two generations of philologists had been trained through the universities and through the *OED*. Men such as William Craigie and C. T. Onions, the editors of the *OED* in Orwell's lifetime, were public figures—the latter so much so that, when he died in 1965, J. R. R. Tolkien called him "one of those people who *were* English at Oxford and at large."[32]

And yet, if anyone *was* English for the popular imagination it was Tolkien himself.[33] His *Hobbit* and *Lord of the Rings* are as much essays in the linguistic as they are in the fantastic imagination. So too was his scholarship. Apprenticed at the *OED* in 1915, he taught at the University of Leeds in the 1920s, and applied in 1924 for the Chair of Anglo-Saxon at Oxford with a statement of his professorial accomplishments. At Leeds, he wrote in his letter for the Oxford professorship, he began with only "five hesitant pioneers" in his course; but soon, his enrollments grew, and his success (he claimed) lay in domesticating something daunting and strange. "Philology," he wrote, "indeed, appears to have lost for these students its connotations of terror if not of mystery."[34]

Philology was a mystery to those who did not know its rules. Even for those who did, there was a kind of magic to its techniques: reconstructing lost sounds through comparison, excavating the dead in their data. Murray himself, in his role as the editor of the *OED* from 1878 until his death in 1915, affected a kind of medieval wizardry in his appearance.[35] Old photographs show him with a long white beard, an old-fashioned academic cap, and a black gown. Contemporary accounts of his demeanor present him as something of a wizard of the word:

> He wore a grey tweed Norfolk suit, and with one hand he grasped his long white beard, as he always did when every cell of the alert brain below the black velvet skull-cap was busy with some great problem.[36]

"Who is that Old Abraham?" an Oxford undergraduate is reported to have asked. His legacy to his profession lay not only in empirical exactitude but in imagination, in creating a persona of word-craft. To be a philologist was to command a social role, a place somewhere between terror and mystery.

The job of the philologist was preservation. Words and their histories needed recording, texts needed editing. The first edition of the *OED* took nearly fifty years to complete. By Orwell's day, it was already in revision.[37] But it was not just a scholarly work. It was a vast social enterprise, built out of a collaborative set of readings, with calls for volunteers to send in examples of words in literary uses. It grew into a "Word Factory," what Murray had called the "Scriptorium," full of shelves with pigeonholes for letters and their words. Well into the twentieth century, and after Murray's death in 1915, the offices of the *OED* sustained what one early visitor had called "the immense forces" and "immense machinery" of its operation.

Reading the story of the *OED* is reading a tale of accumulation. A visitor to its offices noted: "The philological raw material, spread abundantly and heterogeneously, could be ground out by division and sub-division, mechanically, and afterward with reason."[38] The *Dictionary* grew larger and larger, and its Supplements and revisions only added to its bulk. It was a life story of the English language, a "historical monument" (in the words of one of its founders, Richard Chenevix Trench), or in the phrasing of Arnold Bennett in 1928, "the longest sensational serial ever written."[39]

Philology was the business of accretion. In *1984*, it is the business of elimination. "It is a beautiful thing," Syme waxes, "the destruction of words." Here, instead of the many nuanced terms that modify the nouns and verbs of life, there will be but a few core terms and their prefixes: *good, ungood, plusgood*. "Useless shades of meaning" will disappear. Vocabulary will shrink. And works of literature, though they may remain with their authors' names, will change irrevocably:

> The whole literature of the past will have been destroyed. Chaucer, Shakespeare, Milton, Byron. They'll exist only in Newspeak versions, but actually changed into something contradictory of what they used to be. (CW IX: 56)

The point that everybody makes about *1984* is that Newspeak reshapes reality and thought. By dis-enabling nuance, ambiguity, and vagueness, it will leave only "meaning rigidly defined." But what I think has not been said enough about the novel is that imaginative language lies at its center. It is a story of competing writers, a story of individuals striving for agency or, by contrast, striving to efface that agency. The business of philology for the early twentieth century was a business, and for anyone of Orwell's age coming to the *OED* or learning of its making, it would have seemed as vast an enterprise—a bureaucracy of bureau drawers—as anything in social life.

C. S. Lewis was also a product of that world.[40] He was a professional philologist: a professor of English literature and language at Oxford and Cambridge and a fellow Inkling of J. R. R. Tolkien. By the 1940s, he was known for his medieval scholarship in *The Allegory of Love* and his reading of Milton in *A Preface to Paradise Lost*. A theme throughout his writing remains the ways in which words shape social habit and how the nuances of phraseology contribute to a culture's mental landscape. *The Allegory of Love* is about the language of desire. *A Preface to Paradise Lost* is about the rhetoric of seduction. Satan was ever present in the scholar's mind as the manipulator of the word and the orator who could make the ordinary seem magical. "Hell," Lewis quoted his mentor, Charles Williams, "is inaccurate," and for a philologist trained in the niceties of sound-change and semantic shifts, no greater hell could be found than inaccuracy.[41]

Perhaps the most uncannily philological of Lewis's works, however, and the one that resonates most powerfully with *1984*, is *The Screwtape*

Letters. First published in 1942, the book takes the form of a set of letters from a senior demon to his nephew. They have long been seen as part and parcel of the Christian moralism of the author of the Narnia saga, another bit of apologetics of a piece with lions, witches, and wardrobes.[42]

But this is a story of philology, and Screwtape's hell bears more than a passing resemblance to the word factory of the *OED* or Orwell's Ministry of Truth. For deep in subterranean bureaucracy lies the "Philological Arm," a ministry of words designed to lead humans astray by messing up their language. "We have contrived that their very language should be all smudge and blur." That Arm of the devil's state involves destroying words, of rendering the language of the human so oblique and empty as to be virtually useless. As Screwtape writes to his nephew:

> Our Philological Arm has done good work; try the word "complacency" on him. But, of course, it is most likely that he is "living in the Present" for none of these reasons but simply because his health is good and he is enjoying his work. The phenomenon would then be merely natural. All the same, I should break it up if I were you. No natural phenomenon is really in our favour. And anyway, why should the creature be happy?

The medievalist T. A. Shippey, in reviewing Lewis's satanic philology, takes a term out of Tolkien to describe its job, "verbicide"—a coinage transparently connoting word-killing. It is easy to find in Lewis and Tolkien the roots of Syme's love of destroying words. As Shippey puts it, "what Orwell and Lewis saw clearly was that in the modern world, especially and increasingly, language also generated self-deception. In Orwell's terms, 'Newspeak' was vital to 'doublethink.' In Lewis's, the 'Philological Arm' was working to snare the soul."[43] It is a beautiful thing, the destruction of words. Here is Screwtape again:

> The grand problem is that of "unselfishness". Note, once again, the admirable work of our Philological Arm in substituting the negative unselfishness for the Enemy's positive Charity. Thanks to this you can, from the very outset, teach a man to surrender

benefits not that others may be happy in having them but that he may be unselfish in forgoing them. That is a great point gained.

The Philological Arm makes word meaning a matter of use rather than of history. It exposes how certain terms of moral, ethical, or psychological value (complacency, unselfishness) have double edges, easily twisted into something good or bad. Philology becomes the arm of a seductive state, much as in *1984* it will become the instrument of thought control.

Orwell and Lewis never met, but they were close readers of each other's writing. Orwell mentions *The Screwtape Letters* in his largely negative review of Lewis's published BBC lectures, *Beyond Personality*, which he called a "silly-clever religious book" (CW XVI: 437–9). He reviewed, carefully but with reservations, Lewis's 1945 novel, *That Hideous Strength*, in the *Manchester Evening News* (August 16, 1945), thinking its tale of nuclear war mixed with a fantasy of Celtic magic "unfortunate" (CW XVII: 250–1). But Orwell noted, with approval, Lewis's imagination of a National Institute of Coordinated Experiments, "with its world-wide ramifications, its private army, its secret torture chambers, and its inner ring of adepts ruled over by a mysterious personage known as The Head." There is a great deal about Screwtape, or The Head, or almost anyone in Lewis's fictions that eerily anticipates the strategies of *1984*. Screwtape, for example, writes to his nephew that the phrase "living in the present is ambiguous. It may describe a process which is really just as much concerned with the Future as anxiety itself."

By reading *Screwtape* against *1984*, we see not only two polemics but two poetics, two comparable ways of understanding how acts of writing and of reading shape the soul. The philological, for Lewis as for Orwell, is a category not just of academic life but of contemporary culture. Arbiters of words are arbiters of life. By the 1940s, "philological" evoked a culture of lexical legislation, a culture of the *OED* and of the Oxbridge tutorial. Hell may be inaccurate, but Winston's job had been to put those "slips, errors, misprints, or misquotations . . . right in the interests of accuracy." Much like Syme, he is a philologist of the imaginary.

IV.

"It is a beautiful thing, the destruction of words." Linguists may have a social responsibility, but they also have aesthetic judgments, and the moment Syme utters this sentence we know he is doomed. For the great crime in Oceania is not political doubt or moral errancy but aesthetic judgment.[44] Winston's diary entries aspire not just to record events to but shape them. He seeks a novelist's nuance, a sense of finding the right words and phrases. Time and again, he is brought short by beauty, sometimes getting it, sometimes not. Yes, he believes, "the rest of the story had got to be written down." But when he interviews an old prole in a pub, hoping for answers to political and social questions of the past, all he gets is a few tales and some personal accounts. Winston wants facts. The old man gives him story.

And when he steps inside that antique shop he crosses a threshold not just of class but of the literary imagination, a doorway into Dickens. This is as old a curiosity shop as anything in a novel, a house of objects but a house of fiction, too:

> As Winston wandered towards the table his eye was caught by a round, smooth thing that gleamed softly in the lamplight, and he picked it up. It was a heavy lump of glass, curved on one side, flat on the other, making almost a hemisphere. There was a peculiar softness, as of rainwater, in both the colour and the texture of the glass. At the heart of it, magnified by the curved surface, there was a strange, pink, convoluted object that recalled a rose or a sea anemone.
>
> "What is it?" said Winston, fascinated.
>
> "That's coral, that is," said the old man. "It must have come from the Indian Ocean. They used to kind of embed it in the glass. That wasn't made less than a hundred years ago. More, by the look of it."
>
> "It's a beautiful thing," said Winston.
>
> "It is a beautiful thing,' said the other appreciatively. 'But there's not many that'd say so nowadays." (CW IX: 238)

Art is the magnifying glass to life. It makes things larger, brings out detail, enables analogy and simile and allegory. Notice the language of the scene, the constant transformation of a simple object into something in relationship to something else: *almost* a hemisphere, *as of* rainwater, *recalled* a rose or a sea anemone. This is, again, the world of "as if," the world of allusion and association. What is it, Winston asks, but the answer is not so simple. The old man does not define as much as describe it. Winston, instead, gives the true answer. "It's a beautiful thing."

To find something beautiful on the streets of Airstrip One is a crime as deep as any failure of doctrine or dogma. It is the ultimate in thoughtcrime, for it takes a thing of earth and makes it into something else. Aesthetic valuation lives in the simile and metaphor. Newspeak not only cuts out words, it cuts out figures. It proposes a language of the purely literal.

Imagine walking into class and giving students a poem or a piece of prose or snatch of Shakespeare. What is it, you will ask, and you will get familiar answers: it's a sonnet; it's a work of fiction; it's a text; it is a document of social oppression, an artifact of commerce and control; this is the kind of thing that people read a hundred years ago. And you will stand there, silently, and then you'll say: It's a beautiful thing.

What would they say? Where would you have to take your students to make such a response more than risible? You would have to take them outside their classroom, outside their expectations, to a place they'd never been—or if they had, a place they did not really know when they were there. You would have to take them to someplace out of April, some place of memory and desire, but some place no more than a half an hour from the station.

That is where Julia takes Winston. When they meet at Victory Square she gives him directions for their assignation:

> Go to Paddington Station...A half-hour railway journey; turn left outside the station; two kilometers along the road; a gate with the top bar missing; a path across a field; a grass-grown lane; a track between bushes; a dead tree with moss on it. (CW IX: 256)

This is the landscape of desire, the place of memory. It is a place that English readers would have known, but not because they been there in the flesh. They had been there in fiction.

This is Kenneth Grahame country. A half-hour out of Paddington Station, as the train wends along the narrowing River Thames, you'll find villages in which Grahame grew up: Cookham Dean, Quarry Wood, and Mayfield. You'll find the houses and the roads he wrote about. And you will find the riverbank along which he imagined Rat and Mole, the bluebells and the loosetrife and the moss, the grass-grown lanes of *The Golden Age, Pagan Papers,* and *The Wind in the Willows.*[45]

Orwell knew this landscape well. He had been born up the river from London in Henley-on-Thames, and had already drawn on his memories for the novel, *Coming up for Air,* of 1939.[46] There, George Bowling returns to his childhood haunts along the river, remembering the places where he used to fish, finding an old love who cannot remember him, and disappointed that the special places of his life have been overbuilt or covered in trash. He remembers a time when it was "summer all year round," when the "blackberries were getting red enough to eat," and when September brought "sloes and hazel-nuts," "crab-apples." This is the tasty flora of the Valley, the fruits of Grahame country, and Orwell's verbal texture of this landscape owes as much to *The Wind in the Willows* as it does to his own memory.

For there is more to Grahame's influence than the beast fable. Critics who have assessed relationships between the writers see the influence only in *Animal Farm,* especially comparing it to the concluding tensions of *The Wind in the Willows,* when the weasels and the stoats beset the country seat of Mr. Toad and class warfare breaks out within its rooms.[47] But Grahame was everywhere in English literary culture of the first third of the twentieth century, and his impress could be felt by anyone assaying pastorals of memory and desire. *The Wind in the Willows* (first published in 1908) was a famous bestseller, republished and re-illustrated throughout the 1920s and 30s. Grahame's collections of essays from the 1890s were frequently reprinted. *The Cambridge Book of Poetry for Children* (first published during the Great War), became a household text in its revised and expanded editions of the 1930s. Arthur Quiller-Couch included selections from *Golden Days* and *The Wind in the Willows* in his *Oxford Book of English Prose* (1925), selections that made the landscapes of his Thames imagination commonplace even to those who had not read the entire works.

But for those who had, such landscapes were the lens through which to remember not only Grahame's recollections but their own.

When he died, in 1932, eulogies came in from everywhere, most sounding like this letter to the *London Times* from an admirer, the American Kitty Cheatham:

> It was in the springtime when I first met him, when, in answer to a wire, I found myself stepping out of a London train and on to the station platform of the village of Didcot (near Oxford). The platform suddenly disappeared. I found myself in "The Golden Age" facing "The Roman Road" and I began 'a-building...in a dream city where no limitations were imposed and one was sole architect with a free hand.[48]

This was the effect that Grahame's prose had on the popular idiom of the first half of the century—to step out of a station and find yourself in the golden age. "It's the Golden Country," Winston murmurs, as he walks the rural lane with Julia, finding along its stream-banks "a landscape I've seen somewhere in a dream."

Winston may seem to be struck by that landscape, but Orwell was struck by rhetoric. To read Grahame in the first half of the twentieth century was to be affected, again and again, by the sublimity of his prose, with its evocations of delicate landscapes designed to produce a powerful emotional response in their beholders. Take, for example, that richly poetic encounter between Rat and Mole and Pan. When we come to the scene when they have set out to rescue the lost little child of Otter and they boat along a riverbank now filled with music and with spirit, we see the image in the margin and find sanctity in sentiment:

> Slowly, but with no doubt or hesitation whatever, and in something of a solemn expectancy, the two animals passed through the broken tumultuous water and moored their boat at the flowery margin of the island. In silence they landed, and pushed through the blossom and scented herbage and undergrowth that led up to the level ground, till they stood on a little lawn of marvelous green, set round with Nature's own orchard-trees—crab-apple, wild cherry, and sloe.
>
> "This is the place of my song-dream, the place the music played to me," whispered the Rat, as if in a trance. "Here, in this holy place, here if anywhere, surely we shall find Him!"[49]

Now turn to *1984* and find Winston, just off the train from Paddington, deep in Thames Valley country on his way to meet his love:

> Winston picked his way up the lane through dappled light and shade, stepping out into pools of gold wherever the boughs parted. Under the trees to the left of him the ground was misty with bluebells. The air seemed to kiss one's skin. It was the second of May. From somewhere in the heart of the wood came the droning of ring doves. (CW IX: 257)

This is the Grahame pastoral idyll, the return to a literary landscape of the May morning, romance and lyric, filtered through the language of the nineteenth-century aesthetes. The little animals find landscapes covered in "white mist," "pools and pitfalls," and "gold," senses to "kiss the summer back to life," "drones" of insects, and birdsong everywhere:

> Winston looked out into the field beyond, and underwent a curious, slow shock of recognition. He knew it by sight. An old, closebitten pasture, with a foot-path wandering across it and a molehill here and there. In the ragged hedge on the opposite side the boughs of the elm trees swayed just perceptibly in the breeze, and their leaves stirred faintly in dense masses like women's hair. Surely somewhere nearby, but out of sight, there must be a stream with green pools where dace were swimming?
>
> "Isn't there a stream somewhere near here?" he whispered.
>
> "It's the Golden Country—almost," he murmured.
>
> "The Golden Country?"
>
> "It's nothing, really. A landscape I've seen sometimes in a dream." (CW X: 262–3)

It is the landscape not of dream but book, the golden place of Grahame's imagination. "These were golden days," recalls the Sea Rat in his wayfaring story; it was a "golden afternoon" of travel for the animals. What would the lovers find beneath that molehill, or behind the hedge? Would they see, much like Grahame's Rat, "the billowy drapery of beech and elm"? Even that word "surely" takes us back to the verbal politesse of Grahame's creatures: "Surely you have noticed of late"; "now you must surely hear it" (that word, *surely*, shows up sixteen times in the *Willows*). And there must be a stream with green pools. As one twittering bird says to another, "In due time we will be home-sick once more for quiet water-lilies swaying on the surface of an English stream."

Winston and Julia meet in the golden country of a literary childhood. It is an Eden without the Apple, but replete with sexual desire. Grahame's landscape remains, for all its animal emotions, stripped of anything approaching physical arousal (the closest thing to an erotic experience in *The Wind in the Willows* is Mr. Toad's encounter with the rushing motor car). Grahame's sublimities take on, in *1984*, a new eroticism, and the novel's descriptive energies work equally on lovers' bodies as it does on their field.

This is a literary history rewritten, and I have sought to show how Orwell concatenates past textual and linguistic traditions: the allegory of Chaucer and Dante, the realism of Dickens, the philology of the *OED*, the apologetics of Lewis, the precious naturalism of Grahame. There is a growing sense that no text is immune to rewriting, that no author, irrespective of canonical status, stands forever. The most characteristically "Orwellian" version of this view lies, of course, in the novel's appendix:

> A good deal of the literature of the past was, indeed, already being transformed in this way. Considerations of prestige made it desirable to preserve the memory of certain historical figures, while at the same time bringing their achievements into line with the philosophy of Ingsoc. Various writers, such as Shakespeare, Milton, Swift, Byron, Dickens, and some others were therefore in process of translation: when the task had been completed, their original writings, with all else that survived of the literature of the past, would be destroyed. (CW X: 428)

This is a nightmare version of the dream of reading, but it differs only in degree from our experience. For whenever we open up a book, we transform it. Editors translate and transform, bringing texts into line with the philosophy of sixteenth-century reform, Restoration aesthetics, Victorian morality, our own anxieties about coercion and correctness.

Winston's is a world of texts, of scraps of paper, pens, and bound volumes, of "I love you" scrawled on a folded sheet. Like Dante or like David Copperfield, he opens up the book of memory to find a new life or seek heroism on a page. Like Chaucer, he tries to find some sacrality in April dates.

We think of the "Orwellian" as connoting surveillance and surreptition, where official language has been stripped of meaning and the euphemisms of the state place us in some strange otherworld of evasion. We think of Newspeak in the way we think of military codes or campaign rhetoric. This is a facile way of reading *1984*, or any work of literary fiction. What is truly Orwellian about the future is equating authorship with crime, with making literary agency an act of heresy, with decrying the claim that these pages can show me as the hero of my own life.

We want to think that such a future remains far away. But it is here. Philology and criticism take past texts and recast them for a present. Our libraries and classrooms struggle with a dangerous or damning word. In some sense, we are all, like Julia, working in the Fiction Department. And yet, to be alone with a book is to imagine reading stripped of reaction, to place ourselves, again, with David Copperfield in an inherited library. Such an experience is one of the imagination: a way of looking for that little room above the junk-shop where we want to believe there are no telescreens and no one listening. It is a temporary respite. Winston's hideaway is not what it appears; the old antiques proprietor remains an agent. And yet, this is what we want to cherish:

> What mattered was that the room over the junk-shop should exist. To know that it was there, inviolate, was almost the same as being in it. The room was a world, a pocket of the past where extinct animals could walk.

Open the *OED* and think yourself in the Scriptorium with an old wizard. Or take the train out of Paddington a half an hour. Step out from the station and, for a few pages, find yourself in a pocket of the past where extinct animals—a talking Rat and Mole, perhaps—could walk.

Notes

1. All quotations from Orwell's writings are from *The Complete Works of George Orwell*, ed., Peter Davison (London: Secker & Warburg, 1986–98), cited by volume and page number in my text.

2. *OED*, s.v., *Orwellian*, which offers its first appearance from Mary McCarthy's *On the Contrary* of 1950: "A leap into the Orwellian future."

3. David Bromwich, "Euphemism and American Violence," *New York Review of Books* April 3, 2008.

4. On the origins of Newspeak in the "parody" of C. K. Ogden's *System of Basic English* of 1934 and its other potential sources, see Bernard Crick, ed., George Orwell, *Nineteen-Eighty-Four* (Oxford: Clarendon Press, 1984), 430–1. For a broad survey of Newspeak in the context of Orwell's views on language history and change, see. W. F. Bolton, *The Language of 1984: Orwell's English and Ours* (Oxford: Blackwell, 1983). For a review of critical interpretations and cultural assessments of Orwell in general, see John Rodden, ed., *The Cambridge Companion to George Orwell* (Cambridge: Cambridge University Press, 2007). Among the biographical and interpretative materials I have relied on for this chapter are Raymond Williams, *George Orwell* (Baltimore: Penguin, 1971); Peter Stansky and William Abrahams, *The Unknown Orwell* (New York: Knopf, 1972), and *Orwell: The Transformation* (New York: Knopf, 1979); Jeffrey Meyers, *Orwell: Life and Art* (Urbana: University of Illinois Press, 2010); Gordon Bowker, *George Orwell* (New York: Little Brown, 2003); Louis Menand, "Honest, Decent, and Wrong: The Invention of George Orwell," *The New Yorker*, January 27, 2003.

5. Edward Said, *Culture and Imperialism* (New York: Random House, 1993), 209; Christopher Hitchens, *Why Orwell Matters* (New York: Basic Books, 2003), and "Why Orwell Still Matters," in Rodden, ed., *Cambridge Companion*, 201–8.

6. For Orwell at Eton and the literary education it provided, see Stansky and Abrahams, *Unknown Orwell*, and Jonathan Rose, "Englands his Englands," in Rodden, ed., *Cambridge Companion*, 32.

7. The list of "Books Owned" in 1950 has 523 titles (CW XX: 286–99). In his essay "Books v. Cigarettes," *Tribune* February 8, 1946, he states that he had nearly 900 books (CW XX: 287). Many others would have been borrowed or unrecorded.

8. "I am old enough to have been educated at a time when Latin and Greek were only escapable with great difficulty." "As I Please, 32" July 7, 1944. CW XVI: 275.

9. In the 1930s, Orwell wrote to Brenda Salkeld, recommending a collection of "Best Books," including Petronius's *Satyricon* (CW X: 308).

10. Alex Woloch, "Orwell and the Essay Form: Two Case Studies," *Republics of Letters* 4:1 (2014), on line at <http://arcade.stanford.edu/rofl/orwell-and-essay-form-two-case-studies>.

11. *Complete Works of Geoffrey Chaucer*, ed. W. W. Skeat (Oxford: Oxford University Press, 1920), listed in "Books Owned," from which edition I quote.

12. Orwell owned a full run of Eliot's works, including the 1936 edition of the *Collected Poems* ("Books Owned").

13. See Rose, "Englands His Englands," in Rodden, ed., *Cambridge Companion*, 33: "Its opening line echoes that of *The Waste Land* and both employ the same modernist devices; they immediately put the world out of joint, disorient the reader, upset audience expectations with a discordant note, and introduce a mood of indefinable menace."

14. William Hunt, "The Ironic Theology of Nineteen Eighty-Four," *Modern Philology* 110 (2013): 536–63. Hunt's article lays out the specific textual debts to Dante and medieval theological debate, while providing background for the mid-twentieth reception of this historical material for Orwell and his audiences.

15. Orwell left three different editions and translations of Dante in 1950: Dante: *La divina comedia.* 3 vols. Firenze, 1827 (vol. 2 missing); Dante: *Paradiso* [English and Italian], trans. L. Binyon, 1943; Dante, *The Divine Comedy*, Vols II, III. 1948, trans. John D. Sinclair (London: Bodley Head, 1948).

16. No copy of the *Vita Nuova* appears in "Books Owned," but Orwell would have known the text and its literary legacies from a variety of sources: from the widely read translation of Rossetti and from "the Pre-Raphaelite cult of the *Vita Nuova*" in its wake (Nick Havely, *Dante's British Public* [Oxford: Oxford University Press, 2014], 177); from Evelyn Waugh's *Rossetti, His Life and Works* (1929), listed in "Books Owned"; from Eliot's essay "Dante" (published in *Selected Essays* of 1932), where statements such as these bear directly on Winston's writing and reading projects in *1984*: "The *Vita Nuova* plunges us direct into mediaeval sensibility"; "a very sound psychological treatise on something related to what is now called 'sublimation'"; "There is also a practical sense of the realities behind it, which is antiromantic: not to expect more from life than it can give or more from human beings than they can give."

17. See Hunt, "Ironic Theology."

18. On Goldstein's heritage, see the remarks in Crick, ed., *Nineteen Eighty-Four*, 433.

19. Orwell frequently reviewed anthologies and editions, and he often judged verse in editorial terms (for example, "there are music-hall songs which are better poems than three-quarters of the stuff that gets into the anthologies," "Good Bad Books" CW XVII: 347).

20. Norman Ault, *Elizabethan Lyrics from the Original Texts* (London: Longmans, Green, 1925).

21. See Retha Warnicke, "Sir Geoffrey Elton: A Memorial," *History Today* 50 (December, 2004), and Patrick Collinson, "Elton at Seventy," *London Review of Books* 14: 11 (June 11, 1992): 24–5.

22. G. R. Elton, *Policy and Police: The Enforcement of the Reformation in the Age of Thomas Cromwell* (Cambridge: Cambridge University Press, 1972), 3. On the "failure to erase the pope's name from the service books" and the offenses deemed by owning books with the word "pope" in them, see 232, 237.

23. The word "conceal" appears twelve times in *1984*, "concealment" once.

24. Stephen Greenblatt, *Renaissance Self-Fashioning, From More to Shakespeare* (Chicago: University of Chicago Press, 1980), 19, 69, 142, 143, 189, 251, 253.

25. Stephen Jay Greenblatt, *Three Modern Satirists: Waugh, Orwell, Huxley* (New Haven: Yale University Press, 1965).

26. See Shelley Fisher Fishkin, *Was Huck Black?* (New York: Oxford University Press, 1993), and John Alberti, "The Nigger Huck: Race, Identity, and the Teaching of *Huckleberry Finn*," *College English* 57 (1995): 191–37.

27. "Mark Twain—The Licensed Jester" (1943), CW XVI: 5–8.

28. Notice Arthur Conan Doyle, "The Adventure of the Golden Pince Nez" (in *The Return of Sherlock Holmes*, whose 1925 edition Orwell owned): "It was a wild, tempestuous

night, towards the close of November. Holmes and I sat together in silence all the evening, he engaged with a powerful lens deciphering the remains of the original inscription upon a palimpsest, I deep in a recent treatise upon surgery."

29. Orwell himself re-edited Kipling's verse, respelling his dialect representations: "He ought to have seen that the two closing lines of the first of these stanzas are very beautiful lines, and that ought to have overridden his impulse to make fun of a working-man's accent" ("Rudyard Kipling," 1942; CW XIII: 155).

30. A commonplace since Chaucer ("Syth ryme in englissh hat such skarsete," *The Complaint of Venus*, 80). For a chronicle of attitudes towards rhyme in English, see Anne Ferry, *By Design: Intention in Poetry* (Stanford: Stanford University Press, 2008). The concern with lack of rhymes in English was revived in the nineteenth century, often when reviewing literary translations. See, for example, Theodore Watts's review of William Morris's *Beowulf* (*Athenaeum* August 10, 1895, 181–2) on the "paucity of English rhymes," and the comments in the *Harvard Crimson* of November 18, 1891, on Charles Eliot Norton's translation of Dante and "the paucity of rhyme words in English as compared with Italian."

31. Linda Dowling, "Victorian Oxford and the Science of Language," *PMLA* 97 (1982): 160–78, developed further in *Language and Decadence in Victorian Britain* (Princeton: Princeton University Press, 1986).

32. Quoted in Andrew Lazo, "Gathered Round Northern Fires: The Imaginative Impact of the Kolbitar," in Jane Chance, ed., *Tolkien and the Invention of Myth: A Reader* (Lexington: University of Kentucky Press, 2004), 207.

33. See David Lyle Jeffrey, "Tolkien as Philologist," in Chance, ed., *Tolkien and the Invention of Myth*, 61–78; T. A. Shippey, *Tolkien, Author of the Century* (London: Harper Collins, 2000).

34. "To the Electors of the Rawlinson and Bosworth Professorship of Anglo Saxon, University of Oxford," June 27, 1925, in Humphrey Carpenter, ed., *The Letters of J. R. R. Tolkien* (London: George Allen & Unwin, 1981), 12–13, 82.

35. See K. M. Elizabeth Murray, *Caught in the Web of Words: Sir James A. H. Murray and the Oxford English Dictionary* (New Haven: Yale University Press, 1979).

36. Murray, *Caught in the Web of Words*, 298.

37. On the history of the *OED*, see Hans Aarsleff, *The Study of Language in England, 1780–1860* (Princeton: Princeton University Press, 1967); John Willinsky, *Empire of Words: The Reign of the OED* (Princeton: Princeton University Press, 1994); Simon Winchester, *The Meaning of Everything: The Story of the Oxford English Dictionary* (Oxford: Oxford University Press, 2004); Lynda Mugglestone, *Lost for Words: The Hidden History of the Oxford English Dictionary* (New Haven: Yale University Press, 2005).

38. The words of the children's writer and journalist, Jennett Humphries, on her visit to Murray's offices in 1882 and recorded in her essay "English: Its Ancestors, Its Progeny," *Fraser's Magazine* n.s. xxvi (1882): 445.

39. Arnold Bennett, "Books and Persons," *Evening Standard* January 5, 1928.

40. See A. N. Wilson, *C. S. Lewis: A Biography* (New York: Norton, 1990); Chad Walsh, *The Literary Legacy of C. S. Lewis* (New York: Harcourt Brace Jovanovich, 1979); Alastair Fowler, "C. S. Lewis: Supervisor," *The Yale Review* 91 (2003): 64–80, who

remarks that Lewis "valued Orwell very highly" and had "an almost total recall of words."

41. C. S. Lewis, *A Preface to Paradise Lost* (London: Oxford University Press, 1942), 97.

42. Portions of the *Screwtape Letters* were serialized in the Anglican newspaper, *The Guardian* in 1941, before being published in book form (London: Geoffrey Bles, 1942). I quote from the online edition of this text at <http://www.gutenberg.ca/ebooks/lewiscs-screwtapeletters/lewiscs-screwtapeletters-00-h.html>.

43. T. A. Shippey, "Screwtape and the Philological Arm: Lewis on Verbicide," in Jonathan Himes, et al., eds, *Truths Breathed Through Silver: The Moral and Mythopoeic Legacy of the Inklings* (Newcastle: Cambridge Scholars Press, 2008), 119.

44. See his letter to Sir Richard Rees, July 28, 1949 CW XX: 154: "The more I see the more I doubt whether people ever really make aesthetic judgments at all; everything is judged on political grounds which are then given an aesthetic disguise." See, too, Orwell's review of *A Critical History of English Poetry*, Herbert J. C. Grierson and J. C. Smith, in *The Observer* November 26, 1944 (CW XVI: 474–5): "Pound is excluded from mention on what appear to be political grounds."

45. See Peter Green, *Kenneth Grahame: A Biography* (London: John Murray, 1959); Jackie Wullschlager, *Inventing Wonderland: The Lives of Lewis Carroll, Edward Lear, J. M. Barrie, and Kenneth Grahame* (London: Methuen, 1995); Seth Lerer, ed., *The Wind in the Willows: An Annotated Edition* (Cambridge, Mass.: Harvard University Press, 2009).

46. George Orwell, *Coming Up for Air*, in CW VII.

47. Meyers, *Orwell: Life and Art*, 112, convincingly shows how Orwell "tips his hand and slyly hints at his source" in Grahame.

48. I quote from the typescript of the letter in Bodleian Library, Oxford, MS Additional 71217.

49. Lerer, ed., *The Wind in the Willows*, 109.

4

"This Loved Philology"

Poems of the Fall

At just about the same time Orwell was finishing *1984*, the Austrian philologist, Leo Spitzer, having emigrated to the United States and teaching at Johns Hopkins University, delivered one of the greatest tours-de-force of literary analysis Americans had ever heard.[1] In a guest lecture at Smith College, Spitzer reflected on "American Advertising Explained as Popular Art." Using the techniques of close reading, etymological reconstruction, and textual comparison, Spitzer sought to understand the popular, post-War American idiom in literary terms. He focused, in particular, on advertisements for Sunkist orange juice, and he began his lecture by describing a large poster, with a "gigantic glass of juice," a mountain range, an orchard, and a "huge orange-colored sun" (332). In the corner of this poster were the words (aligned here as Spitzer aligned them):

> From the sunkist groves of California
> Fresh for you

The lecture was soon published, and in thirty pages of dense, heavily footnoted scholarly prose, Spitzer revealed this seemingly straightforward ad as a poem of the cultural imagination. He opened up the resonances of the word "sunkist," explored the grammar of the phrasing, compared its imagery to classical and Renaissance poetry, and, exfoliating from this technical analysis, reflected on the very nature of American mythology. "In the city drugstore, over whose counter this sunny picture shines, the wall opens up before us like a window on to nature" (333). The selling of a glass of juice becomes an ad for American imagination: a point at which commerce and beauty meet. "Business becomes poetic," Spitzer states, "because it recognizes the great grip which poetry has on this modern unpoetic world" (334).

What grip does poetry still have? For Spitzer—lecturing after a decade of exile; conscious, like so many of his European colleagues, of the dispersal of European intellectual culture; seductive and patronizing, at the same time, to his privileged American college audience—America imagined itself as a place of "Arcadian beauty" (334), truly a new world with its landscape physically untouched by bombing, trenches, shells, and gas. The groves of California, he claims, may in fact exist; but that is not the point here. The point is that advertising sells a fantasy rather than a reality, an ideal rather than a fact. "The better world which the advertiser evokes is a never-never land." This is what Spitzer calls a vision of a "paradisiac world filled with fragrant groves where golden fruit slowly ripen under the caress of the sun." The audience for this ad makes an imaginative "detour through this *word-paradise* and carries back the poetic flavor which will season the physical enjoyment of the orange-juice." Poetry, he concludes, has established here "a realm of pure, gratuitous, disinterested beauty" (345–7).

Spitzer's essay has been seen as a marvel of a literary mind, an arabesque of brilliant intuition, and perhaps the first example of what would become the tradition of "cultural studies" in American universities. He picked a shard of common life and read it as if it were a lyric of St. John of the Cross. And yet, to get behind the pyrotechnics of his reading is to find something that speaks to any writer on tradition, old or new. It is to recognize that ours remains a search for origins; that any notion of tradition or of history implies a starting point; and that our readings and responses seek to return us to someplace special, someplace before we had fallen into business or to avarice, someplace like paradise before the apple. Spitzer's story is as much a story of temptation as it is of interpretation. "Fresh for you": the phrase, he recognizes, invites the reader. Take it, drink it, here, it is good for you.

How can we not hear, behind these words, a much older tempting with a piece of fruit? How can we not read, in Spitzer's self-conscious phrasing, a sense of the complex challenges that beauty poses: the relationships between tasting and knowing, between memory and desire? His is as much a Miltonic as a mercantile meditation on the beautiful and the sublime. Drink this, and you will be transported back. Eve listened to the serpent, and she bit into the apple. So did, on her urging, Adam. So do we.

This sense and this sensation of taste bring me back to origins. I have already noted how the critic Denise Gigante has scripted the afterlife of this Miltonic imagination as a history of taste, a story of how literary understanding and cultural value grow, at least in part, out of our conflicted experiences of that first bite.[2] "The Miltonic fall," she argues, "involves more than epistemological or moral errors of judgment: it also involves a kind of judgment inextricable from pleasure. That taste involves pleasure is a lesson the Romantics learn from Milton and that we learn from Romanticism" (2).

If we think of taste as the exercise of judgment in the service of aesthetic response, then certainly that first bite in the story of human kind is a critical as well as moral act. The story of Adam and Eve—as filtered through the Bible and its literary transformations—is a story of taste: of finding for the first time not only the knowledge of good and evil but the savor of what pleases the tongue:[3]

> Eve, now I see thou art exact of taste,
> And elegant, of Sapience no small part,
> Since to each meaning savour we apply,
> And Palate call judicious; (*Paradise Lost* IX. 1017–20)

Savour and *Sapience*: the wordplay rings in the ear. The pun on knowing and tasting had been one of the great tricks of Latin literature, and Milton plays on it as well. But this not simply a fall into knowledge or sin. It is a fall into criticism. Adam treats Eve as a late seventeenth-century reader would treat a work of art or literature. His words— *exact, elegant, judicious*—had become the key terms in an emerging discourse of judgment.[4] Adam becomes a knowing connoisseur of an arousing beauty ("now I see"), a philologist of desire. And when he looks Eve in the eye he does not simply take her hand. He seizes it, and in that action makes the acts of tasting, knowing, and appreciating something carnal.

If this is a fall into a kind of carnal criticism, it is a fall, too, into language itself. At this moment, according to centuries of theological and scholastic argument, language itself changed. On his creation, Adam could name all the creatures of the earth, and each name corresponded exactly with its thing. What scholars would call "the language of Adam" was a vocabulary of essentials. There was only one name for each thing, and one thing for each name. But with the Fall,

all that was lost. Words became estranged from the things they denoted. Literal expression became figurative. "The fall," wrote Norman O. Brown, "is into language."[5] And in that second fall of Babel, as St. Augustine recognized, the diversity of human tongues only further alienated us from each other and the world. *Linguarum diversitas hominem alienat ab homine.* This is the world in which we live, a world in which words no longer mean, exactly, what we think they should; a world in which intention and expression divide us; a world in which language has become something we put on, like fig leaves, to hide our fears.[6]

This chapter traces a poetic tradition that tries to comprehend the Fall as a fall into literature and criticism. It looks at some American poets possessed by the unrecoverable pastness of the past, of memory as a search for meaning. It turns to the traditions of philology as an attempt to grapple with that sense of loss. This is what Spitzer tried to do: to comprehend how signs became estranged from things, how words could represent not real-life landscapes but a never-never land; how the experience of beauty, joy, or pleasure gained by looking at the advertisement, buying the juice, and drinking it all grant some knowledge to the reader. Taste involves pleasure. But it also involves pain, a sense that what we taste is a memory we never had, that in the biting of the apple or the drinking of the orange juice, we recognize how much we live in landscapes of imagination and desire.

I.

No American poet so transformed the landscapes of taste and temptation as much as Emily Dickinson.[7] In her dazzling brief stanzas, she brought together everything from personal reflection, to natural observation, to biblical allusion, Miltonic grandeur, and local idiom—all compressed into hymn-style verse that scans, almost obsessively, like prayers. Dickinson, scholars have revealed, was no mere isolate. The old picture of her sitting, lonely in her Amherst, Massachusetts upstairs, composing her strange poems, seeing no one, has been replaced by a recognition that she was as much a person of the world and of the book as of her room.

She read widely, and Noah Webster's *Dictionary of the American Language* (with its literary quotations and pithy definitions) was a constant companion. She owned her father's copy of the 1844 edition of the *Dictionary*, and scholars have revealed how she checked meanings and found collocations among words as she wrote her own poems.[8] She wrote to her friend and mentor Thomas Higginson, in April 1862, "for several years, my Lexicon was my only companion." In that same letter she tells him of her favorite books: "For Poets—I have Keats—and Mr and Mrs Browning. For Prose—Mr Ruskin—Thomas Browne—and the Revelations."[9]

Dickinson's father, she continued, "buys me many books—but begs me not to read them—because he fears they joggle the mind." How her mind must have been joggled by Keats's "Ode on a Grecian Urn," with its famous concluding injunction: "Beauty is truth, truth beauty,—that is all / Ye know on earth, and all ye need to know." Amid the hyphens of her prosody, we see these phrases reconfigured in some of Dickinson's most powerful lines:

> I died for Beauty – but was scarce
> Adjusted in the Tomb
> When One who died for Truth, was lain
> In an adjoining Room –
>
> He questioned softly "Why I failed"?
> "For Beauty", I replied –
> "And I – for Truth – Themselves are one –
> We Brethren, are", He said –
> And so, as Kinsmen, met a Night –
> We talked between the rooms –
> Until the Moss had reached our lips –
> And covered up – our names –

Poetry such as this may constitute as much a reading of the literary tradition as any work of literary criticism. It takes Keats's equation between Beauty and Truth and turns it into a dialogue among the dead. It takes the knowledge of the two and makes it not a knowledge needed here on earth but something buried in the ground. It takes Keats's lines and uses them as provocation for a different kind of inscription, the names of the dead, soon covered by the creeping moss.[10]

This is a poem not of eternal verities but of unceasing change. Moss covers stones and voices fail. Dickinson saw America constantly changing. The railroad and the Civil War altered irrevocably its fields and forests. And yet, reared on a language of belief stretching back to the Puritans, Dickinson often commented on the tensions of a new world gone bad. One of her last datable poems, for example, transforms almost into parody the famous "Cradle Song" of Isaac Watts—a poet who had been a mainstay of the Anglo-American devotional imagination:

> Now I lay me down to sleep
> I pray the Lord my Soul to keep
> And if I die before I wake
> I pray the Lord my soul to take.

Watts's straightforward address has the feel of naïve belief. It is a poem of verities, a poem that affirms the order of the world in the Lord's hands. Here is Dickinson's version:

> Now I lay thee down to Sleep –
> I pray the Lord thy Dust to keep –
> And if thou live before thou wake –
> I pray the Lord thy Soul to make –

She has turned prayer into address. The first person becomes the second person. Sleep here is no temporary respite from the world but now the sleep of death. The speaker lays a body to its final rest; ashes to ashes, dust to dust. And in the weird rewriting of the last two lines, Dickinson images something of a necromancy of desire. The Lord makes souls, and if the addressee lives before waking—if it should come to live again—then let it be a life of the soul with the Lord.[11]

Dickinson constantly takes us into these bizarre worlds of life-in-death, of looking back to something pleasant and finding in it something horrid. That word "horrid" is a word she uses with profound effect in one of her best-known poems, a unique synthesis of learned allusion with everyday observation.[12]

> I like to see it lap the Miles –
> And lick the Valleys up –
> And stop to feed itself at Tanks –
> And then – prodigious step
>
> Around a Pile of Mountains –
> And supercilious peer
> In Shanties – by the sides of Roads –
> And then a Quarry pare

To fit its sides
And crawl between
Complaining all the while
In horrid – hooting stanza –
Then chase itself down Hill –

And neigh like Boanerges –
Then – prompter than a Star
Stop – docile and omnipotent
At its own stable door –

The poem describes a railway train, moving along its track, stopping for water, hooting down through trestles and tunnels, until it finally rests at its station. First, the train seems like a cat. Noah Webster, in his *American Dictionary*, defined the word *lap* as "to take into the mouth with the tongue; to lick up; as a cat laps milk." To illustrate his definition, he quotes Shakespeare's phrase, "cat laps milk." Webster had put "lap" and "lick" together—a collocation, like so many others, that inspired Dickinson. But what turns this lexicography to poetry is yet another level of recall: Milton. Here is Satan, in the serpent's form, coming to Eve:

> Oft he bow'd
> His turret Crest, and sleek enamel'd Neck,
> Fawning, and lick'd the ground whereon she trod.
> (*Paradise Lost* IX: 525–7)

There is something almost Satanic about this great train. It is *prodigious*, and Webster quotes Thomas Browne: "It is prodigious to have thunder in a clear sky." There is the noise of the thundering train, a noise that calls to mind Boanerges, the name that the Gospel of Mark gave to the Apostles James and John and meaning "sons of thunder." There is a growing sense of greatness here, but, too, a sense of pride. Look up the word *supercilious* in Webster and you will find, "lofty with pride." We ride now not on iron rails but lines of poetry, and if the poet's own stanzas aspire to great metaphor, so too, the train speaks in its "horrid – hooting stanza." *Horrid*, is for Webster, a distinctively Miltonic word. He quotes the phrase "horrid sympathy," but horrid is everywhere in *Paradise Lost*. It means bristling in an awful, terrifying way, and the word shows up eighteen times in Milton's poem. Phrases such as "horrid confusion," "horrid fray," "horrid strides," and "breaking the horrid silence" could not be far from Dickinson's imagination here, and her poem ends with a concatenation of Miltonic echoes: her "punctual as a Star" recalls (through Webster's own quotation) Milton's description of the earth as "this punctual spot"; and her "omnipotent" train, now stopping like a frothing horse at its stable door, brings up the warnings, repeated throughout *Paradise Lost*, against defying the "Omnipotent" Lord.

The train laps up the countryside much as the poet laps up miles of meter, feeding on older verse. These tastes are both amazing and disturbing: marvels of technology and, yet, strangely horrid and destructive. Much as the railway cuts through mountains, rocks, and quarries, so too a little snake will make its path through grass:

> A narrow fellow in the grass
> Occasionally rides;
> You may have met him—did you not
> His notice sudden is,
> The grass divides as with a comb,
> A spotted shaft is seen,
> And then it closes at your feet,
> And opens further on.
>
> He likes a boggy acre,
> A floor too cool for corn,
> But when a boy and barefoot,
> I more than once at noon
> Have passed, I thought, a whip lash,
> Unbraiding in the sun,
> When stooping to secure it,
> It wrinkled and was gone.
>
> Several of nature's people
> I know, and they know me;
> I feel for them a transport
> Of cordiality.
> But never met this fellow,
> Attended or alone,
> Without a tighter breathing,
> And zero at the bone.

This poem offers the flip side of the train poem. Instead of great, we have small. The snake does not pare a quarry but splits, narrowly, the grass. But there is more here. "Narrow" does not mean simply thin. It connoted, for mid-nineteenth-century America, something confining and constrained. Satan, in *Paradise Lost*, finds himself in "narrow" places, and "sudden" appearances proliferate throughout Milton's poem, much as they do here, to amaze the viewer. We would like to think that we are not in Milton's Eden but America itself. And yet the "Boggy Acre" and the "floor too cool for Corn" take us back, again, to *Paradise Lost*: the former, echoing the "Boggie Syrtis, neither Sea, / Nor good dry Land" through which Satan travels on his way to earth; the latter recalling the "plenteous crop / Corn wine and oyle" that Adam and Even should reap from the soil.

We like to think, too, that Dickinson speaks in her own voice here, but she seems to not. This is a man's memory, recalling when he was "a Boy and Barefoot" coming upon the snake in the sunlight. The man recalls trying to capture an old feeling; he reflects on his knowledge of the natural world, and his respect and ease in it. And then he ends by stating that the snake still makes him fearful. "Zero at the bone" has become a catchphrase for terror now.[13] Its brilliant metaphor compresses a world of fear into a narrow space. But if it contains multitudes, it also splits us off. Riven from humanity, much as the snake divides the grass, we end this poem not attended but alone. As Milton repeatedly reminded us, Eve was, to her mate, "flesh of my flesh, bone of my bone" (the phrase appears four times in *Paradise Lost*). Dickinson's speaker now becomes some old Adam, recalling a time of barefoot pleasure, recognizing that there is no company of flesh, but only zero at the bone.

Dickinson's poetry is full of such allusiveness, such complex recastings of literary traditions. It takes us to the heart of the American mythology explored by Leo Spitzer: a mythology of that "paradisiac world filled with fragrant groves where golden fruit slowly ripen under the caress of the sun." Poetry has a "great grip" on "this modern unpoetic world," and Dickinson consistently juxtaposes the poetic and the technological, the imaginary and the everyday—as if to restore something that had been lost, as if to bring back a poetic imagination to a fallen landscape:

> Of Paradise' existence
> All we know
> Is the uncertain certainty –

> But its vicinity infer
> By its Bisecting
> Messenger –

What could that "bisecting messenger" be but the narrow fellow who divides the grass as with a comb? It is as if we live, in Dickinson's world, always *after* something; as if hers are poems of remembrance, trying to make sense out of traditions of belief that barely hold us, still. "Heaven" she wrote (the word is in her own quotation marks) "is what I cannot reach!" and she continues:

> The Apple on the Tree –
> Provided it do hopeless – hang –
> That "Heaven" is to me.

To read these lines against those of her other poems and through Leo Spitzer's vision of American "word-paradise" is to see, as the critic Robert Weisbuch has seen, a poetry that brings together "religion... [and] consumer culture."[14] "Come slowly, Eden," she enjoins in another poem, watching a bee go for nectar, and in another she looks back on language itself as a kind of Edenic space of understanding:

> A Word that breathes distinctly
> Has not the power to die
> Cohesive as the Spirit
> It may expire if He –
> "Made Flesh and dwelt among us"
> Could condescension be
> Like this consent of Language
> This loved Philology.

All you need to do is open Dickinson, almost at random, and you will find poems that present this fall into language. The very word "condescension" literally means a stepping down, what Webster called in his *American Dictionary* "voluntary descent from rank." This is not so much a Fall as it is a voluntary descent, and Dickinson sees of the word made flesh as something of an incarnational philology. For in her final line, she takes the etymology of "philology" (what Webster called "a love of words") and recapitulates, makes it "loved" and loving in itself. Heaven is what I cannot reach: in quotation marks, "heaven" is less a place than a word itself, a sign of something that we try to understand, something we try to reach for past the apple on the tree.

II.

For Robert Frost, reaching for heaven in an apple tree remains a story of the poet's quest to get back to an original meaning through the scrim of literary tradition.[15] As in Dickinson, words hearken back to other words; Milton is there, Shakespeare, and Dickinson herself, and for all of Frost's late-life faux-naïve public pronouncements, the poetry he published in the 1910s is as allusive and sophisticated as anything in print anywhere.

After Apple-Picking

My long two-pointed ladder's sticking through a tree
Toward heaven still,
And there's a barrel that I didn't fill
Beside it, and there may be two or three
Apples I didn't pick upon some bough.
But I am done with apple-picking now.
Essence of winter sleep is on the night,
The scent of apples: I am drowsing off.
I cannot rub the strangeness from my sight
I got from looking through a pane of glass
I skimmed this morning from the drinking trough
And held against the world of hoary grass.
It melted, and I let it fall and break.
But I was well
Upon my way to sleep before it fell,
And I could tell
What form my dreaming was about to take.
Magnified apples appear and disappear,
Stem end and blossom end,
And every fleck of russet showing clear.
My instep arch not only keeps the ache,
It keeps the pressure of a ladder-round.
I feel the ladder sway as the boughs bend.
And I keep hearing from the cellar bin
The rumbling sound
Of load on load of apples coming in.
For I have had too much
Of apple-picking: I am overtired
Of the great harvest I myself desired.
There were ten thousand thousand fruit to touch,

> Cherish in hand, lift down, and not let fall.
> For all
> That struck the earth,
> No matter if not bruised or spiked with stubble,
> Went surely to the cider-apple heap
> As of no worth.
> One can see what will trouble
> This sleep of mine, whatever sleep it is.
> Were he not gone,
> The woodchuck could say whether it's like his
> Long sleep, as I describe its coming on,
> Or just some human sleep.

We have often wanted to see Frost as the celebrant of simple things, the poet of a uniquely American pastoral. But from the start of this poem, we are not grounded in familiar earth but reaching up to air. Heaven is what I cannot reach. Frost's speaker here abandons the ladder to heaven, tired of his aspirations. What is left after apple-picking is the recognition of our own humanity. We sleep just as humans, and what Dickinson would have called "Nature's people" no longer can speak to us directly. Were he not gone, the woodchuck could say something. But such a creature has disappeared, and in this landscape we could not understand him even if he did speak.

All reaches up to heaven are reaches to poetry, and Frost and Dickinson share a self-consciousness about the literary process. Dickinson is always writing about writing—not in a self-referential or indulgent way, but in a way that shows us (to paraphrase Spitzer) how, in this new and unpoetic world, poetry must be the business of our lives. There is a loved philology to Frost as well, and "After Apple-Picking" tells a story of attempting to make literature out of life.

For Frost had always seen his poets in the landscape. Writing to Susan Hayes Ward from England in September 1912, he noted how, living in Beaconsfield, he had planted himself securely in the loam of the English literary tradition:

> Here we are between high hedges of laurel and red-osier dogwood, within a mile or two of where Milton finished *Paradise Lost* on the one hand and a mile or two of where Grey lies buried on the other and within as many rods or furlongs of the

house where Chesterton tries truth to see if it wont prove as true
upside down as it does right side up.[16]

Old landmarks on the road are like a bookshelf, each one recalling a
past author. And, later in life, those authors seemed never too far from
Frost's imagination. In a notebook entry from the early 1920s, he
writes:

Exact knowledge + some judgment and taste versus exact
knowledge.[17]

It is as if he is trying to distill Milton's new-fallen Adam into an
equation, trying to discern the true relationships between taste and
knowledge. Eve, now I see. Exactly.

But in "After Apple-Picking," that sight is unclear. The poem's narrator picks up an icy sheet from the surface of the farm trough. It is
already something else, a pane of glass. Frost shows us, at this moment,
that the poet's fallen eye sees things as metaphors. He does not say,
I skimmed a sheet of ice that looked like a pane of glass. We must
infer, and in that inference lies our understanding of what poetry
does. Poetry is the ice-sheet through which the world now looks
strange. Unlike real glass, it melts as soon as it is touched; it breaks
and falls. Before it does so, we may be provoked to dream. "After
Apple-Picking" is a poem of such falls, a poem about what it means to
live in language and aspire to a heaven of poetic prowess.

The apples are not tasted here. They are smelled and touched,
heard and seen. All but one of the senses are in play, and the absence
of what apples taste like in this poem stands in sharp contrast to other
scenes of tasting fruit in *North of Boston* (the 1914 volume in which
"After Apple-Picking" first appeared). The poem "Blueberries" begins
with the narrator amazed at the size and beauty of the berries he sees
on a walk. "You ought to have seen what I saw," he opens, but his
interlocutor has no idea where he has seen these fruits. The two go
back and forth, until the second speaker realizes that blueberries can
grow quickly, just about anywhere. And the first speaker affirms:

> It must be on charcoal they fatten their fruit.
> I taste in them sometimes the flavor of soot.

The story goes on: does the farmer know those berries are there? Is
"any fruit to be had for the picking"? And then, "If he thinks all the

fruit that grows wild is for him / He'll find he's mistaken." Finally, when the speaker resolves to return to the pasture, he recalls what things looked like:

> You ought to have seen how it looked in the rain,
> The fruit mixed with water in layers of leaves,
> Like two kinds of jewels, a vision for thieves.

"Blueberries" is a story of temptation. What happens when you come upon ripe fruit? Should you ask whose it is? Should you just take it? This poem offers a kind of prelude to "After Apple-Picking"—a story of imagining a "cavernous pail" full of fruit, a story of anticipation. But, only a few pages later in this volume, fruit is picked and done, the great harvest never living up to expectation. I am overtired.

So, too, perhaps, was William Carlos Williams. Frost's poetic contemporary, Williams pared his language down to powerful imagery. Many of his poems are like little notes left on the kitchen tables of the everyday.

> This is Just to Say
>
> I have eaten
> the plums
> that were in
> the icebox
>
> and which
> you were probably
> saving
> for breakfast
>
> Forgive me
> they were delicious
> so sweet
> and so cold[18]

Like Frost's "Blueberries," this is a poem about coming upon fruit that is not yours. But here, the fruit gets eaten. This is less a performance than it is a letter, remorse turned to writing. I've plucked forbidden fruit. This is a bit of text acutely aware of style and look and devoid of punctuation. Here, the only capital letter, other than the first "I," is the one that begins the word "Forgive." Like Frost's apple-picker or like Milton's Adam, Williams's scribbler is a critic. He makes judgments of aesthetic value. This is a poem of and about taste itself. Its longest word is the word "delicious," a word that takes us back to Milton, where "delicious taste," "delicious fruit," and "delicious vines" tempt Eden's couple (the word "delicious" appears ten times in *Paradise Lost*). Delicious fruit had tempted Emily Dickinson, too: "I wish you could have some cherries," she wrote to her brother Austin in June 1851, "they are very large and delicious."[19] And in the early summer of 1873, she wrote to Mrs. J. G. Holland that she never believed "Paradise...to be a superhuman site"; "Eden" she said, "seemed" always eligible, especially this day in the sunshine and especially with birds singing:

> To what delicious Accident
> Does finest Glory fit![20]

The plums in Williams's icebox have a literary heritage. But by the time he published this poem in 1934, the word "delicious" had taken on a new and commercial meaning. Ever since the first years of the twentieth century, "Delicious Apples" were a marketed variety, and American advertising of the first third of the twentieth century was full of invitations to take a bite.[21] One fruit crate label from before the Second World War shows a bright red and yellow apple, with "DELICIOUS FRUITS" above them, and in script: "Quality Apples from the Hills of Kentucky."[22] Much like Spitzer's orange juice ad, this label tempts us with an Eden of good taste, now not the groves of California but the hills of Kentucky. It practically shoves the apples in our face. Together with its bold typography, this picture revels in what Spitzer called the "optimistic confidence" of an American faith in "a world-order in which Nature works for the good of the individual man" (356). And yet, what happens when an individual disrupts that order? Forgive me. Williams's poem tells a little tale of fracturing and then trying to mend the order of things. Here, fruit does not hang tempting from a tree, but it has been already picked, cold in the icebox. His is a poem not of the grove but of the kitchen, a poem (to adapt Spitzer's phrasings) offering "a colorful image...to refresh the city dwellers in their environment of hustle and drabness" (356). Delicious fruits: how can we not rise to the invitation?

III.

What all these poets recognized, and what Spitzer so brilliantly analyzed, is that America is a land of taste. The tongue is both the site of
savoring the world and the instrument of speaking about it. Williams's
title, "This is Just to Say," reminds us that when we open our mouths,
we may take in a flavor and report its pleasure. Much as the first man
and woman will transgress against an all-seeing divinity, so poets often
frame their confrontations with temptation against figures of authority.
Reading Emily Dickinson's poems through her letters makes you powerfully aware of Thomas Higginson as her ideal reader. Frost's early
poems seem addressed to some compelling demiurge, and Williams's
brief verse, now in the kitchen of the imagination, reads like Adam's
note taped to God's fridge.

America's first poet, Anne Bradstreet, already had these figures
down.[23] She was the daughter and the wife of men who had founded
the Massachusetts Bay Colony, who had served as its governors and
who participated in the founding of Harvard College. Sailing to
America (already married) at eighteen in 1630, she arrived with eight
hundred of her own books, and by the time she began writing poetry
she was as well-read as anybody could have been in early New England.
She mentions, quotes, or alludes to Hesiod, Homer, Thucydides,
Xenophon, Aristotle, Virgil, Ovid, Quintus Curtius, Pliny, and Seneca.
And those are just the classics. She drew heavily on Joshua Sylvester's
popular translation of the sixteenth-century French poet Guillaume
Du Bartas. She knew the writings of Sir Walter Raleigh and contemporary translations of Plutarch. She wrote an elegy on Philip Sidney
and drew on a wealth of contemporary historical and devotional writers for poetic meditations on the elements, the seasons, the ages of
man, the spirit and the flesh, and old and New England.[24]

Scarcely a line of her verse misses an allusion, and her poetry is
powerfully concerned with establishing an individual (and individual
woman's) voice in a tradition of male writers, fathers, and husbands.
From many of her sources—Puritan theology, the Bible, and Du
Bartas's poetic treatments of Creation—she cobbled together a poetic
understanding of what it means to start anew in a new world. A literate
colonial Eve, Bradstreet addresses many of her poems to a male
authority, whether he be her historical parent or husband, or her gov-
ernor or God.

Her book, *The Tenth Muse,* was originally printed without her permission in 1650 (a fellow colonist had sailed to England with a manuscript of her verse), and she set about to oversee her own authorized, printed collection. She died in 1672, but in 1678 her *Several Poems* appeared from a Boston printer.

Bradstreet begins her book by addressing two fathers: first, her own one, Thomas Dudley; second, her poetic one, Virgil. In both she is concerned with beginnings and lineages. She limns the contours of traditions both familial and literary, first by locating her address in terms of "Adams Race," and second by framing her aspirations against Virgil's story of the fall of Troy and founding of Rome. "To sing of Wars, of Captains, and of Kings, / Of Cities founded..." These are things too "superior" for her. Instead, she writes of everyday things, and throughout her verse, the domesticities of birth and death, of home and husband, all aspired to be as sweet as the rhetoric of antiquity.

For it is in that idiom of sweetness that Bradstreet brings together taste and knowledge, language and desire. Poets, from antiquity onwards, had been perceived as "honey-tongued." Sweet music and sweet verse are such commonplaces, now, that we strain to see the metaphor of taste behind them. But for Bradstreet (as for her contemporary, Milton), it was always there. Her "Prologue" poem mentions the "sugard's lines" of the seventeenth-century poet Du Bartas; the "sweet consort" of viol music; the "sweet tongue'd Greek" of antiquity. All contribute to a poetics of taste here. And if the woman's place is secondary to the man's—if, as Bradstreet humbles herself before what "men can do best"—nonetheless, her rewards are potentially as flavorful. "Give Thyme or Parsley wreath, I ask no bayes." In lieu of the laurel of poetry, she requests, give me a wreath of kitchen herbs.[25]

Bradstreet works closely in the traditions of theological debate and dogma of her age. But a poem such as "The Flesh and the Spirit" seems to anticipate the eerie dialogues of Dickinson or the farm-hand colloquies of Frost:

> Sister, quoth Flesh, what liv'st thou on –
> Nothing but Meditation?
> Doth Contemplation feed thee so
> Regardlessly to let earth goe?

And Spirit replies:

> Be still thou unregenerate part,
> Disturb no more my settled heart.

...

> How I do live thou need'st not scoff,
> For I have meat thou know'st not of:
> The hidden Manna I doe eat,
> The word of life it is my meat.

Like Truth and Beauty in the tomb, the Flesh and Spirit offer a seminar on what makes life worth living. Like the two yokel interlocutors in "Blueberries," they have an argument about what feeds the soul. Eating is everywhere, and the imagery of Bradstreet's poem (deeply indebted to generations of theological discussion) could be the imagery of any devotional writer. But read in the context of her whole book, it is clear that she is offering a new poetics of ingestion: a poetics of the taste and the temptations of life in this new world. "The Dialogue between Old England and the New" has the old country talk about a "Physick puring potion, I have taken," and when New England responds, her question "is 't Intestine wars that thus offend?" takes on a positively alimentary feel. We read on, and find New England's attempt at consolation: "You are my Mother Nurse, and I your flesh, / your sunken bowels gladly would refresh."

Throughout her poems, divine and historical characters are eating, drinking, and tasting. Her verses on the four elements have Earth speak of the "sundry fruits my fat soil yields.../ Their kinds, their tasts, their colors & their smells." Her poem on the ages of Man has Middle Age speak of longing "to tast on Royalty." And her poem on the four seasons has Summer report of "fruitful Crop" as richly and as tastily as anything from Milton to Williams:

> Now's ripe the Pear, Pear-plumb and Apricock,
> The prince of plumbs, whose stone's as hard as Rock
> The Summer seems but short, the Autumn hasts
> To shake his fruits, of most delicious tasts...

This is poetry of the sensorium of the emerging American imagination. Words such as "sweet," "fresh," and "beauty" fill her lines. She plays on *savor* and *sapor* as brilliantly as Milton (Old Age says "I cannot scent savours of pleasant meat, / Nor sapors find in what I drink or eat"). There is as much fruit hanging in her poetry as in Frost's own New England, and her apples tempt as much as his. "Pear, and Plum, and Apple-tree now flourish," and "Apples now their yellow sides do show." But behind all of them lies one forbidden fruit. For sometimes, she writes, when a man thinks back on past events, he may imagine himself in Eden:

> Sees glorious Adam there made Lord of all,
> Fancies the Apple, dangle on the Tree,
> That turn'd his Sovereign to a naked thral.

What Bradstreet learned from all her teachers—fathers, husbands, writers, poets—was that to remember is to sense a loss. The Puritan experience was always an experience of self-examination. But more than that, it was a sense of living in an elegiac world. That elegiac quality was everywhere: in the poems and memorials on the young children, prematurely dead in Massachusetts winters; in recollections of that loss of Eden after eating of the apple.

My work on Bradstreet here recalls my study of the Puritan environments for early American children's literature.[26] For what the Puritans knew well was that childhood itself provoked the elegiac. All children's stories recall a lost past, an age before adulthood. All children die—they must, for to become a grownup, the child must move on. Seventeenth- and early eighteenth-century children's literature ripples with these images, and Bradstreet's poetry, for all its thrills of composition, always seems to mourn. Her grandchildren died young. Her house, with all her books, burned to the ground in the summer of 1666. Even so, we can remember:

> When present times look back to Ages past,
> And men in being fancy those are dead,
> It makes things gone perpetually to last
> And calls back moneths [*sic*] and years that long since fled.

Only in our imaginations can the dead come back. Only in recollection does tradition have a meaning. To return to Emily Dickinson's aphoristic epiphany, "Today, makes Yesterday mean." To be a poet conscious of tradition is to be a poet not just sensitive to the past but sensing the present. Bradstreet has an observant eye, captivated by the smells and tastes of field and orchard, and yet constantly reminding herself that "The word of life it is my meat."

IV.

How do we find a meaning in a single word? Must we inquire in the dictionary and thus make our lexicon our only friend? Must we ask fathers, mothers, and teachers for our definitions? And when do we recognize that words change meaning; that the literal or lexical only suffices in the covers of a book, and that in common speech things live in figures, similes, and allusions?

The American poet Gjertrud Schackenberg assesses all these questions in her well-known poem, "Supernatural Love," originally published in 1985 and now a staple of classrooms and anthologies:[27]

> My father at the dictionary-stand
> Touches the page to fully understand
> The lamplit answer, tilting in his hand
>
> His slowly scanning magnifying lens,
> A blurry, glistening circle he suspends
> Above the word "Carnation." Then he bends
>
> So near his eyes are magnified and blurred,
> One finger on the miniature word,
> As if he touched a single key and heard
>
> A distant, plucked, infinitesimal string,
> "The obligation due to every thing
> That's smaller than the universe." I bring
>
> My sewing needle close enough that I
> Can watch my father through the needle's eye,
> As through a lens ground for a butterfly
>
> Who peers down flower-hallways toward a room
> Shadowed and fathomed as this study's gloom
> Where, as a scholar bends above a tomb
>
> To read what's buried there, he bends to pore
> Over the Latin blossom. I am four,
> I spill my pins and needles on the floor

Trying to stitch "Beloved" X by X.
My dangerous, bright needle's point connects
Myself illiterate to this perfect text

I cannot read. My father puzzles why
It is my habit to identify
Carnations as "Christ's flowers," knowing I

Can give no explanation but "Because."
Word-roots blossom in speechless messages
The way the thread behind my sampler does

Where following each X I awkward move
My needle through the word whose root is love.
He reads, "A pink variety of Clove,

Carnatio, the Latin, meaning flesh."
As if the bud's essential oils brush
Christ's fragrance through the room, the iron-fresh

Odor carnations have floats up to me,
A drifted, secret, bitter ecstasy,
The stems squeak in my scissors, *Child, it's me,*

He turns the page to "Clove" and reads aloud:
"The clove, a spice, dried from a flower-bud."
Then twice, as if he hasn't understood,

He reads, "From French, for *clou*, meaning a nail."
He gazes, motionless. "Meaning a nail."
The incarnation blossoms, flesh and nail,

I twist my threads like stems into a knot
And smooth "Beloved," but my needle caught
Within the threads, *Thy blood so dearly bought,*

The needle strikes my finger to the bone.
I lift my hand, it is myself I've sewn,
The flesh laid bare, the threads of blood my own,

I lift my hand in startled agony
And call upon his name, "Daddy, Daddy"—
My father's hand touches the injury

As lightly as he touched the page before,
Where incarnation bloomed from roots that bore
The flowers I called Christ's when I was four.

With its carefully controlled iambic pentameters, its chiming three-grouped rhymes, and its arresting tensions between syntax and rhythm generated by its enjambments, "Supernatural Love" emerges as a poem brilliantly in dialogue with literary tradition. At the most basic level of the poem's plot, the young girl tries to understand her father's lexicography, his sensibility of word and definition. He is reading. She is doing needlepoint. Because she's only four, her needlework is awkward, and she slips and pokes herself. Blood runs from her finger, and her father touches the wound to try to heal it.

At the verbal level, however, there is much more going on here than a childhood reminiscence. Schnackenberg looks back on the legacies of American verse. Bradstreet's learned father hovers over hers. A loving parent and a loving God seem, somehow, intertwined, and if Bradstreet had taken up the pen instead of the needle, Schnackenberg remembers a time before she could read or write, when the needle was her only instrument of craft. "Who says my hand a needle better fits?" asked Bradstreet. And yet, here, the girl lives through the needle, looking at the world through its eye, stitching words in its X's on the frame. Her needle moves through the word, until it slips and moves through her finger. The Christian imagery of blood and salvation looks back to those deep American traditions of devotion, and in an Eden populated only by the fragrant flowers in a dictionary, daddy comes to touch the injury much as he would touch the page.

Carnation/Incarnation. The poem trades on brilliant wordplay, what Emily Dickinson had called "loved philology," and there is much that takes us back to Dickinson as well. Words such as "tomb" and "bone" recall her famous poems on Beauty and Truth and the snake. But, more broadly, the story of the little embroiderer takes us back to a story of a young girl, much in love, whose cheeks redden like a rose, whose speech "staggers":

> Her fingers fumbled at her work –
> Her needle would not go;
> What ailed so smart a little maid
> It puzzled me to know.

Love flowers in the woman's face, much as it flowers on the dictionary's page, and if "Supernatural Love" imagines daughterhood among a dictionary reader, so too we must recall Dickinson with her father's copy of Webster, looking for yesterday's meanings.

But if we start the poem over, we can now see Frost among its iambs. The scanning magnifying lens through which her father reads recalls that frozen pane of glass through which the apple-picker views the world. The father's is a "magnifying lens," and Frost's narrator dreams of "magnified apples." "I feel the ladder sway as the boughs bend." The father "bends/ So near his eyes are magnified and blurred." And as the little girl twists her "threads like stems into a knot," we see the flower stems of her father's dictionary flowers come together with "stem end and blossom end" of Frost's dreamer.

"Supernatural Love" remains a poem of so many things—love, memory, fear, learning, devotion—that it takes rereading to unravel all its threads. The philologist in me looks for its story of "word-roots," how behind every etymology there lies a tale, a romance of return. "I cannot read," the poet remembers herself as a girl. But I can, and I read anew the sense of sacrifice and sacredness in loving through the word. I am a scholar bending above a tomb to read what is buried there. But literary history is more than just a parade of the dead. As Bradstreet noted, every reminiscence makes them come alive. The root of every word, in the end, may be love. Certainly, as my book has tried to show, each act of reading takes us back to childhood memory. We may love literature, not simply for its entertainment or its teaching but for its ability to take us back to times we can just barely recollect. David Copperfield recalls his boyhood in the library; Orwell remembers reading Dickens's novel as a nine-year-old. And Gjertrud Schnackenberg, like some American Miranda speaking to her distracted Prospero, imagines an age before reading, before writing, before the letter itself, when a girl's instrument was not a pen but a needle. The tensions of this poem bristle as we read it against a history of seemingly willful subordination to a man: as Bradstreet sees her father and her husband as her tutors; or as Dickinson would sign herself to Thomas Higginson as "Your Scholar" and "Your Pupil."

In speaking to his audience at one of America's premier women's colleges, Leo Spitzer must have been well aware of the seductions of his speech. His playful self-effacements belie his assurance: "things

American, ... with which my listeners will be much more familiar than I"; "I know nothing about the genesis of the particular advertisement to be discussed"; "To adopt a resentful or patronizing attitude toward our time is, obviously, the worst way to understand it" (330–1). But Spitzer always loved to play both with and to his listeners. We know from documents and memoirs that he acted the role of the great professor to the hilt. His colleague Erich Auerbach called him "full of activity and tactlessness ... very cordial, very malicious, very presumptuous, very insecure, very sentimental, ... a born comedian."[28] We know that, in exile in Istanbul in the late 1930s, Spitzer made trouble for his Turkish hosts, challenging their uneasy relationship with the German authorities in the city. He blew up, at one point, over the maltreatment of a Jewish musician, and wrote a long, enraged letter to the German vice counsel. He went on for a full page, and then ended: "This is what I wanted to say; forgive my openness."[29]

It is a small step to hear Spitzer's varied voices in the lecture on American advertising. And it is a small step to hear him riffing on the allegories behind orange juice, boldly telling this post-War, women's college audience that a "basic mistrust of language itself ... is one of the most genuine features of the Anglo-Saxon character" (348), or that "Americans know reality so well" (349) or that "Americans are the most Cartesian of peoples" (352), and then remember: "This is what I wanted to say; forgive my openness."

If poetry exists to be made out of this most unpoetic world, it is by writers and critics who recognize what they must say, but at the same time ask forgiveness. Spitzer and Williams would not have known of each other in the 1930s, but it comes uncannily to me to hear avowals of saying and forgiving in both. It seems to me that, even as an Austrian Jew in exile, Spitzer recognized the tensions between action and apology that would so motivate an American poetic tradition of the Fall. A father figure at the dictionary-stand, he makes us all his pupils and his daughters.

It is those children who transform tradition. Every student will remake the canon and its contexts with each reading. Every bite into the fruit gives them a taste of past and present. Schnackenberg's girl will lift her hand "in startled agony." But how many of our students cut themselves on the spiky point of literature? How many of them leave class, bleeding in disbelief? Spitzer may have sought applause from his audience. But I would rather have a single hand raised, startled.

Notes

1. Leo Spitzer (1887–1960) began his career in Marburg and Cologne, Germany, before leaving in 1933, first for Istanbul, then Johns Hopkins University. See Hans-Ulrich Gumbrecht, *Leo Spitzers Stil* (Tubingen: G. Narr, 2001), and Kader Konuk, *East West Mimesis: Auerbach in Turkey* (Stanford: Stanford University Press, 2010). Spitzer's lecture, "American Advertising Explained as Popular Art," was delivered at Smith College in 1948 and originally published in *A Method of Interpreting Literature* (Northampton: Smith College, 1949), 102–49. I quote from the reprinting in Alban K. Forcione, Herbert Lindenberger, and Madeline Sutherland, eds, *Leo Spitzer: Representative Essays* (Stanford: Stanford University Press, 1988), 327–56.

2. Denise Gigante, *Taste: A Literary History* (New Haven: Yale University Press, 2005).

3. Quotations from Milton's works are from John T. Shawcross, ed., *The Poetry of John Milton* (New York: Anchor Books, 1971).

4. The *OED* cites this passage to illustrate *exact*, adj, def. 2, "Of persons: Highly skilled, accomplished, (in taste) refined," and its next quotation is from Alexander Pope's translation of the *Odyssey*, "Two sew'rs…Exact of taste." "Elegant," too, is defined as a matter of "good taste," and by Milton's time it had come to refer to literary language tastefully arranged. "Judicious" came to be associated with discerning and discriminating critical taste, often in discussions of painting, poetry, and theological interpretation.

5. Norman O. Brown, *Love's Body* (Berkeley and Los Angeles: University of California Press, 1966), 257.

6. St. Augustine, *The City of God Against the Pagans*, vol. VI, ed. and trans. William Chase Greene (Cambridge, Mass.: Harvard University Press), Book XIX, chapter vii, 148–9.

7. I use Thomas H. Johnson, *The Complete Poems of Emily Dickinson* (Boston: Little Brown, 1960). Influential criticism includes Shira Wolosky, *Emily Dickinson: A Voice of War* (New Haven: Yale University Press, 1984); Sharon Cameron, *Lyric Time: Dickinson and the Limits of Genre* (Baltimore: Johns Hopkins University Press, 1981); Christanne Miller, *Emily Dickinson: A Poet's Grammar* (Cambridge, Mass.: Harvard University Press, 1989); Robert Weisbuch, "Prisiming Dickinson; or, Gathering Paradise by Letting Go," in Gudrun Grabher et al., eds, *The Emily Dickinson Handbook* (Amherst: University of Massachusetts Press, 1998), 197–224.

8. See Jed Deppman, "'I could not have defined the change': Rereading Dickinson's Definition Poetry," *The Emily Dickinson Journal* 11 (2002): 49–80, and The Emily Dickinson Lexicon, online at http://linguistics.byu.edu/faculty/hallenc/EDLexicon/nehgrant.html.

9. Emily Dickinson, Thomas Herbert Johnson, and Theodora Ward, *The Letters of Emily Dickinson* (Cambridge, Mass.: Harvard University Press, 1986), 404.

10. See Virginia Jackson, *Dickinson's Misery: A Theory of Lyric Reading* (Princeton: Princeton University Press, 2005).

11. See Victoria N. Morgan, *Emily Dickinson and Hymn Culture: Tradition and Experience* (Farnham: Ashgate, 2010).

12. My discussion of this poem develops and recasts material originally presented in Seth Lerer, *Inventing English: A Portable History of the Language* (New York: Columbia University Press, 2007), 188–9.

13. A Google Books search as of August 2015 shows eight novels or memoirs with the title *Zero at the Bone* published since 1991.

14. Weisbuch, "Prisiming," 200.

15. I have been most influenced by Richard Poirier, *Robert Frost: The Work of Knowing* (New York: Oxford University Press, 1977), Jay Parini, *Robert Frost: A Life* (New York: Henry Holt, 1999), and William Logan, *Our Savage Art: Poetry and the Civil Tongue* (New York: Columbia University Press, 2010), and "The Other Other Frost," *The New Criterion* 13 (1995): 21–6. Quotations from Frost's poetry are from Edward Connery Lathem, *The Poetry of Robert Frost* (New York: Henry Holt, 1979). Quotations from the notebooks are from Robert Faggen, ed., *The Notebooks of Robert Frost* (Cambridge, Mass.: Harvard University Press, 2006). Quotations from the letters are from Donald Sheehy, Mark Richardson, and Robert Faggen, eds, *The Letters of Robert Frost, Volume 1: 1886–1920* (Cambridge, Mass.: Harvard University Press, 2014).

16. Frost to Susan Hayes Ward, September 5, 1912, in *Letters*, 67, 70.

17. *Notebooks*, 275.

18. A. Walton Litz, Jr., and Christopher MacGowan eds, *The Collected Poems of William Carlos Williams, Volume 1: 1909–1939* (New York: New Directions, 1986), 372.

19. *Letters of Emily Dickinson*, 119.

20. *Letters of Emily Dickinson*, 508.

21. *OED*, s.v., *delicious*, def. 2. b. For a review of the term "delicious" in the apple's cultivation and advertising history, see Adrian Higgins, "Why the Red Delicious No Longer Is. Decades of Makeovers Alter Apple to Its Core," *The Washington Post*, August 5, 2005. For an account of the supposed "discovery" of the Delicious variety in the early 1900s, see the interview in the Charleston (West Virginia) *Daily Mail* of October 18, 1962, at <http://www.wvculture.org/HISTORY/goldendelicious02.html>.

22. See the reproduction at <http://www.antiquelabelcompany.com/store/DELICIOUS-FRUITS-Brand-apple-fruit-crate-box-art-lithographed-label-Framed-p120.html>.

23. See Jeannine Hensley, *The Works of Anne Bradstreet* (Cambridge, Mass.: Harvard University Press, 1967); Cheryl Walker, *The Nightingale's Burden: Women Poets and American Culture before 1900* (Bloomington: Indiana University Press, 1982); Luke Spencer, "Mistress Bradstreet and Mr. Berryman: The Ultimate Seduction," *American Literature* 66 (1994): 353–66; Kimberly Latta, " 'Such is My Bond': Maternity and Economy in Anne Bradstreet's Writing," in Susan C. Greenfield and Carol Barash, eds, *Inventing Maternity: Politics, Science, and Literature 1650–1865* (Lexington: University Press of Kentucky, 2015), 57–85.

24. See Kevin J. Hayes, *A Colonial Woman's Bookshelf* (Knoxville: University of Tennessee Press, 1996), 16–17.

25. A search of the *OED* for the phrase "parsley wreath" suggests that Bradstreet got the phrase from Sylvester's English translation of Du Bartas. The *OED* also quotes from Luke Spenser's critical account in "Mistress Bradstreet": "At the end of the prologue, Bradstreet asks not for bays but only for a humble, housewifely thyme or parsley wreath as recognition of her worth."

26. See Seth Lerer, *Children's Literature: A Reader's History from Aesop to Harry Potter* (Chicago: University of Chicago Press, 2008), 81–103.

27. Originally published in *The Lamplit Answer* (New York: Farrar, Straus and Giroux, 1985), reprinted in *Supernatural Love: Poems 1976–1992* (New York: Farrar, Straus and Giroux, 2002), and included in such anthologies as *The Norton Anthology of Modern Poetry* (New York: Norton, 1996), and Mark Strand and Eavan Boland, eds, *The Making of a Poem: A Norton Anthology of Poetic Forms* (New York: Norton, 2000).

28. Erich Auerbach, letter to Ludwig Binswanger, March 3, 1930. For the German original, and the impact of this judgment in the larger context of Spitzer's reputation among the scholarly community of pre-War Europe, see Seth Lerer, "Auerbach's Shakespeare," *Philological Quarterly* 90 (2011): 21–44, esp. 36–8, 43.

29. See Kader Konuk, *East West Mimesis*, 107.

5

The Tears of Odysseus

In Book 8 of Homer's *Odyssey*, the poem's hero finds himself washed up on fresh shores of community and culture.[1] Alcinous, his host on this well-governed island of the Phaeacians, welcomes the stranger, and orders a set of entertainments for his honor. Commanding that a feast be set, Alcinous also commands the singer, Demodocus, to appear "to give delight in whatever way his spirit prompts him to sing" (VIII.45). And so, before the slaughtered sheep and boars, the minstrel sings the tales of Troy. He sings, first, about the quarrel of Odysseus and Achilles. Odysseus, moved to tears at the tale, hides his face in his cloak. There are further entertainments: games and contests, trials of archery and racing. Again Demodocus sings, and now he tells the story of Ares and Aphrodite, cuckolding her husband, Hephaestus. Then, gifts are exchanged, Alcinous's daughter appears, and Odysseus turns to the great feast and cuts off one of the choice portions of the roasted kill and gives it to the singer. "Come now," he asks, "and sing of the building of the horse of wood...the horse which once Odysseus led up into the citadel as a thing of guile" (VIII.490–5). Demodocus obliges, and Odysseus now, his heart melted and his tears wetting his cheeks, cannot conceal how moved he has been from his host. Like a woman keening over dead kin, we are told, Odysseus weeps. And Alcinous, similarly moved, beseeches his strange guest to tell his name, to tell his story. "Tell me the name," "tell me of the people," "tell me why." To these requests, Odysseus will answer. He will become his own best poet, "Odysseus, son of Laertes, known among men for all manner of wiles," and for the next three books of Homer's poem he holds his Phaeacian audience, and us, spellbound with stories of the Lotus Eaters and the Cyclops, the Laestregonians and Scylla and Charybdis, Circe's isle and the underworld, and finally his nine years with Calypso.

This is the turning point in the *Odyssey*: the moment when narrative catches up with itself, when the hero gets to tell his story to a captive audience, and when, in the figure of Demodocus, we get to see the poet himself, perhaps, imagining his own social position. Scenes such as these compel us to imagine the performances of Homer's stories long before they had been written down. They invite us to think of singers who sang to their audiences, to reconstruct the ways in which adventures of a hero find themselves transformed into public literature.[2]

These are scenes, too, of direct and unmediated literary response. Face-to-face at the feast, Odysseus weeps as Demodocus sings. There is, here, an immediacy of effect, for nothing stands between the teller and the listener. The scene goes on in real time, in the lines it takes to tell the story and the moments of response. And Odysseus, hearing the stories of his comrades and himself, does not interpret, does not gloss, does not explain. He simply cries.

Many of my students long to cry as he does. Often, as high-school teenagers or undergraduates, they come to literature because they want this face-to-face experience of character and action. They respond well to the lived presence of a classroom teacher, the personality and vividness of his or her performance. At times, they think of fiction as if it were fact and personalize the non-existent. What would Emma do? What happens to Pip after the end of Dickens's novel? What was it like for Hamlet growing up in Elsinore? The school experience trades on the lecture and the lectern. It invites students to engage directly with the text, unmediated by bibliography or criticism or generations of interpretation. What do you think? becomes the default question of the introductory classroom.

My students may come wanting Homer, but I often given them Virgil. For all my presence as a teacher, when I'm questioned I give bibliography. For all my aspirations as a lecturer, I tell my students what to read. I give them not a Homeric but a Virgilian experience: an experience of literacy and mediation, a story of allusions, empire, and effort. The *Aeneid* is very different from the *Iliad* and *Odyssey*. It offers no scenes of direct or unmediated literary engagement. Instead, it gives us an always-interpreted reflection on the crafts of word and object, of the echoes of power behind the poetry. If Homer represents, in my conceit, the needs of students, Virgil presents the model for professors.

Let me explain. Aeneas weeps in Virgil's poem, but he does so at different things and in different ways.[3] Drawing explicitly on Homer's presentations of the epic hero welcomed at a strange court, Virgil has Aeneas greeted at Queen Dido's Carthage. He tours the great building projects of the city and looks over its artistic shows. On one wall, he sees, as a mural, a pictorial representation of the fall of Troy. He marvels at the handiwork of artists, and sees the wars, the battles, and the players in the city's fall. He stops. He weeps. "With many tears and sighs he feeds / his soul on what is nothing but a picture."

Book I of the *Aeneid* introduces its hero not as a listener but a reader. The tales of Troy are not presented but re-presented. They are in pictures, artistically formed. Aeneas does not hear but see. He sees *inani pictura*, an empty picture, signs and symbols he must register and understand. In the course of the Book, Aeneas does identify himself to Dido and her court. He does sit to a feast and hear a blind bard sing of old things. And he does, in Books II and III of the *Aeneid*, tell his own story in his own way. But in Virgil, everything is different. His characters are shapers of artistic tales. They are as literate as he and his own audience had been, and the scenes of teaching in the *Aeneid* differ markedly from those of the *Odyssey*. Aeneas's pedagogic guide to the underworld in Book VI is the Sybil, an interpreter of cryptic signs. She reads the scattered leaves, and offers teachings in which truth is wrapped up in obscurity. Later in that book, when Aeneas finds his own father among the blessed dead, it is a father who comes off as a schoolroom lecturer, giving a lesson on Platonic theories of the soul and, then, offering a history of what will happen in the Rome that Aeneas will found.

Little wonder that the late Antique and medieval scholars of the *Aeneid* read it as an allegory of education.[4] The fifth-century North African scholar, Fulgentius, understood the first six books of the poem as one long colloquium, with the poet leading the reader through the byways of interpretation. Virgil appears, here, as a schoolmaster, "with a preoccupied frown and notebooks held ready to start some new composition." He teaches that, in the guise of a history, he has presented a story of study: in the Latin of the treatise, a *gradus*, or set of steps for learning. This Virgil traces out his hero's growth. In Book I, he is speechless, like a newborn baby. In Books II and III, he is diverted by the stories. Book IV finds him distracted by passion, Book V honoring his father, and Book VI finally ready for formal instruction by the Sybil and his father.

To read the *Aeneid* in this way is to find the hero as a student. Subsequent allegorists, such as Bernardus Silvestris and John of Salisbury, in the twelfth century, made much of this approach. Book VI, in their accounts, was the most explicitly pedagogical of the books, and they saw the content of the *Aeneid* less as a political story of founding a city or a romance of desire and distraction than as a body of philosophical argument about the nature of the soul and its passage through life.

By the time Homer was rediscovered, in his Greek, in the European sixteenth century, these allegorical readings were passing out of fashion. New fascinations with the place of epic poetry in large imperial projects were displacing old obsessions with the schoolroom and its obscurities. By the eighteenth and early nineteenth centuries, Homer and Virgil were increasingly "historicized": read for what they illuminated of their own times, located in their pasts, and edited in an attempt to restore their originals.[5] In the process, they became the two poles of European literary origins. Nations needed their formative epics, and the search for long, great poems in the languages of Europe sought to find versions of these authors for new nations. *El Cid* for Spain, *Beowulf* for England, the *Nibelungenlied* for Germany, *The Song of Roland* for France: these were the poems that were elevated to the status of great, formative epic statements for their respective readers. And in the history of literary reception, Chaucer, Dante, Shakespeare, Milton were all, at some point, dubbed the Virgils of their age.

They were dubbed so not only because of their foundational relationship to literary forms and national traditions, but because they were all viewed as teachers. Scenes of reading, writing, lecturing, and grading fill their works, sometimes literally and sometimes figuratively. All of them present, in various ways, figures of authority that teach and judge. Virgil makes Dante his best pupil, as the *Inferno* becomes one long subterranean seminar. *The Canterbury Tales* presents its exemplary stories as forms of instruction on its roadside classroom. Adam, in Milton's *Paradise Lost*, becomes a model student for the angels who instruct him.

In all of the works I have explored here, there is a pedagogical imperative. Betsey Trotwood teaches David Copperfield how to interpret Mr. Dick. Montag's superiors instruct him in the arts of literary destruction. O'Brien leads Winston Smith through the byways of the Party. And Leo Spitzer stands as guide to the American experience, his readings of the past and present echoed in the history of poetry of taste and fall. Like Schnackenberg's father at his dictionary, I lift my finger from the page to try to make things whole.

Implicit in my book has been an idea of what makes literature "literature": of what distinguishes a certain kind of writing from another, of what makes certain books matter to us. Literature "teaches" because literary words embed scenes of teaching in their fictions. Books teach us how to read them, and their scenes of explicit instruction place us in the classroom of their learning.

In the *Iliad* and the *Odyssey*, we have examples of the primary epic: presentations of performance, tales of direct encounter and response. In his *Mimesis*, Erich Auerbach identified these features of the "Homeric style" as follows: "to represent phenomena in a fully externalized form, visible and palpable in all their parts, and completely fixed in their spatial and temporal relations" (6). "Homer can be analyzed," Auerbach noted, "but he cannot be interpreted" (13). This is, of course, not to say that Homer's poetry cannot be read and understood through the techniques of critical study. It is to say, however, that Homer's literary fictions do not offer us a model for their literate and critical interpretation.

In Homer's poetry (with perhaps only one, enigmatic example), there are no representations of writing or symbolic communication.[6] Everything is face-to-face, spoken, and direct. Scenes of literary performance are scenes of singing and listening. When Auerbach says that Homer cannot be interpreted, what he implies is that the stories of the Homeric past cannot be taken for anything other than what they are. The only response to such stories is emotive, rather than intellectual. Odysseus weeps.

Aeneas weeps as well, but it is weeping of a different sort. There, it is the felt response to acts of reading and interpretation. Everyone, in fact, is interpreting in Virgil's poem. When Dido, for example, turns to her sister in Book IV, she asks the meaning of these strange and moving dreams that beset her at night. When she and Aeneas, later in the book, eventually consummate their desire in a cave in a thunderstorm, she understands it as marriage; he does not. The characters in Virgil constantly ask what a moment means. So too, must we.

Much of our university literary study is, in this sense, Virgilian. It trades on writing, rather than reading. It privileges mediation. One version of it has gone so far as to argue against any unmediated literary experience to show that all forms of literary understanding are the products of histories of reading. It is at times explicitly political, finding in character and action allegories of empire. It is at times attentive to disparities of gender (Dido as a figure of female literary subjectivity) and geography (what does it mean to come from Africa or Asia and find power in the West?). It is about translation and transmission: stressing a self-consciousness of historical reading, not just across languages, but across classrooms, as we come to the past already encrusted with generations of teaching. It is about the mastery of bibliography, about criticism and commentary. "What do you think?" cannot be asked until the student knows what someone else has thought.

At the heart of these distinctions is the nature of immediacy. A Homeric experience is one of an immediate response. We hear, we feel. By contrast, a Virgilian experience is one of mediation. It privileges the delay in response. It argues for resistances: resistance to immediate feeling, resistance to the immediate experience of understanding. "Literature," then, becomes intimately bound up with notions of immediacy, and immediacy is one of the central principles of study. How readers confront the relationships between immediacy and delay of meaning constitutes a theory of reading and a practice of teaching.

My classroom practice and my scholarship has helped me understand the ways in which our felt response to literature is often delayed or impeded by the very structures of the literary works we study. But my work has also helped me grasp that, whatever the individual response to literature may be, the social function of the act of literary study is the building of communities of reading.

My work in children's literature has argued that we need to understand this form not as an isolated genre (fantasy, fairy tale, adventure) or as the product of specifically calibrated authors (literature intended for children), but as the history of reading and reception. Children's literature is what children read, whether or not it was originally written for them. At different times and in different cultures, children were reading Homer and Virgil, Chaucer and Shakespeare, Swift and Defoe. They were reading the Bible, writing in their prayer books and

Psalters, underlining in their novels. My claim throughout my work has been that children's literature in the West takes as its primary goal an education in the arts of literacy: a way of showing that the book is a world and the world is a book; a way of seeing how the ABC's of primers offer allegories of experience; a way of seeing signs in everyday experience. The schoolroom, the library, the desk, and the page are the places of the literate imagination, and my understanding of the social function of "literature" hinges on the idea of bringing children into shared experience around a text.

A history of children's literature thus parallels a history of education. Key moments in works of fiction come when children find themselves in libraries or studies: for example, when Jo March finds herself in her uncle's private library; when Johnny Tremaine heals his hand while reading in his doctor's study; when Hermione Granger susses out the secrets to success in the Hogwarts library. Wizardry, in *Harry Potter*, is but another form of literacy—much as, in the Middle Ages and the Renaissance, alchemy was really nothing but a heightened form of literacy, making recipes, reading lists of ingredients, developing a patter while you duped the populace. When I teach Chaucer, I inform my students that this is the whole point of Chaucer's *Canon's Yeoman's Tale*, that strange story of an alchemist and his apprentice, coming almost out of nowhere towards the close of the Canterbury pilgrimage and so full of arcane learning that the plot itself appears to disappear behind its verbiage. Alchemy is just another kind of literary fiction. Take the detritus of our lives and turn it into gold. The storyteller is a master alchemist. So is the teacher who can turn the seeming dross of distant texts into glittering classroom revelation. Just as the paintings of old alchemists show them invariably with their books, so, too, the writer and the teacher rely on the texts that guide them.

But to what end? Is our purpose just to tempt or entertain? Is it to teach straightforward lessons of morality or ethics or communal value? Should I content myself with those student evaluations that, year after year, patiently record all I've tried to show, all of my learning on display, and all my eloquence, distilled into an all-too-frequent seeming praise: "made dull material interesting."

As I have read and taught, the most effective distillation of the goal of education comes to me not from a poem or a novel or a work of literary criticism but from a guide to raising children. Towards the close of Dr. Benjamin Spock's *Baby and Child Care* (first published in 1946), the chapter, "What is School For?" avers:

> The main lesson in school is how to get along in the world. Different subjects are merely a means to this end...You learn only when things mean something to you. One job of a school is to make subjects so interesting and real that children want to learn and remember.[7]

Behind this statement is a functional definition of teaching that argues for the classroom as a site of socialization. Content is secondary to experience. Dr. Spock's claim that "you learn only when things mean something to you" is not a transparent claim for personal relevance. It is recognition that our modern condition is one of individual engagement and recall. The German scholar Harald Weinrich had said something similar when he remarked that "For moderns, recollection...is a privatized kind of memory....Recollections are therefore always in principle 'my' recollections."[8] And, much as T. S. Eliot would blend memory and desire into his own claim for a pastness to the past, so Dr. Spock sees meaning as inseparable from wanting. "One job of a school is to make subjects so interesting and real that children want to learn and remember." One job of literature is to find, and then remake, things so interesting and real that we *want* to read and recall what we read.

The function of literary study is to create sites of socialization for purposes of positive community development. Literary works that narrate experiences of learning can be used to illustrate the very problem of the classroom: that is, as I have presented it, the tension between immediacy and estrangement. Literary works are often valued for their ability to make things "interesting and real." We could even argue that one definition of "the canon" is precisely that collection of works that correspond to socially defined criteria of interest and realism. Our bookshelves, as much as our class schedules, are made up of those who make things interesting.

I.

Let me try.

The differences between Homer and Virgil are, of course, historical as well as pedagogical. For while our text of the *Odyssey* comes down to us after generations of literate and scholarly ministrations, it was most likely, in its origins, an orally performed work. It is this very "orality" of Homer that has spurred a view of ancient epic as precisely living in the face-to-face, and Demodocus's performances may represent some version of the old Homeric world of telling tales to a responsive, and responding, audience. Virgil, by contrast, is not simply writing for a literate and literary readership. He is continuously representing acts of literate interpretation: the reading of pictures on a wall, of augeries in the sky, of enigmatic signs and symbols. Homer and Virgil represent the historical and the social differences in public poetry and its reception. The near-millennium or so between them spans the distance between an age of hearing and an age of reading.[9]

For later cultures and societies, however, differences between the "oral" and the "literate" were not so clear-cut. During the English Middle Ages, for example, much poetry (whether it was composed in writing or not) was orally performed, and there is evidence that many of our best-known lyrics, songs, and lays had a long life in circulation before they were written down. The life of Geoffrey Chaucer straddled these arenas of the popular, the courtly, the oral, and the written. Many of his poems were most likely read aloud to listening audiences. Some of them may have been only read in private by a literate few. If any writer has a reputation for making dull material interesting—and if any writer has articulated the self-consciousness of doing so—it is Chaucer.

His *Canterbury Tales* explicitly dramatizes both the literary and the social tensions between oral performance and literate reading.[10] Chaucer takes as his central literary fiction the idea that his is a set of oral performances, offered in lived time, by carefully limned characters before a present audience. Such *Tales* as those told by the Miller or the Nun's Priest or the Wife of Bath have an immediacy about them: a sense that we are genuinely listening to and with, that we are in the moment of the telling.

This is, of course, completely imaginary. *The Canterbury Tales* is a carefully crafted, continuously revised work of literate and literary poetry. Its lines are far too full of learning to be given to its pilgrims (would the Miller really know Cato? Would the Wife of Bath really know Ovid?). There is the ongoing premise of oral performance, especially when the drunken Miller interrupts the Knight. But there is the fact of a literate readership. For when Chaucer's narrator turns to his audience and begs forgiveness for recording the Miller's lewd tale, he asks his *readership* to skip it, if they wish:

> And therfore, whoso list it nat yheere,
> Turne over the leefe and chese another tale;
> For he shal fynde ynowe, grete and smale,
> Of storial thing that touchesth gentilesse,
> And eek moralitee and hoolynesse.
> Blameth nat me if that ye chese amys.[11]

> And therefore, whoever does not want to hear this story,
> Turn over the leaf and chose another tale,
> For he shall find plenty of things, important and trivial,
> Such as historical writings concerning courtly behavior,
> And also works of morality and holiness.
> Don't blame me if you chose wrongly.

Writing at a time of change in literary history and literary language, working in English poetry from French and Latin models, and creating verbal art not for a commissioning aristocratic patron but for a potentially wide, urban and urbane readership, Chaucer hits precisely on the challenges of author and audience, feeling and fiction. He recognizes that our acts of literary understanding are both shaped by the media of their transmission (in this case, a bound manuscript) and by the desires of the audience. We can pick and choose. The author offers us a plate of options. Do not blame him if you chose wrongly.

Such choice remains unavailable to those in face-to-face experience. Odysseus cannot stop Demodocus just because he weeps. He may ask for a story in particular—the wooden horse—but once the taleteller begins, it would be both aesthetically and socially wrong to stop him. Odysseus cannot turn the page.

We can. But do we wish to? Would any of us truly skip a story so anticipated as the Miller's? Would any of us take at face value the author's claim that, if we wish, we truly can read in the order that we wish? Of course not. How can we not turn to the *Miller's Tale*? It has a plot that holds our interest, a setting of palpable material reality, and characters whose motives seem transparent. There is vividness to physical description and linguistic performance. The Miller himself is a detailed character: brusque, interrupting, drunk, carnal. His Nicholas is cleverly manipulative; his Alisoun bodily seductive; his Absolon narcissistically effete; his John the Carpenter hilariously opaque. The story brilliantly resolves itself around the prospect of the flood, the kissing of the private parts, and the poetic justice of just desserts for all.

Many modern readers enjoy this *Tale* for its immediacy of action and response. By contrast, they dislike—some even find inexplicable—the *Tale of Melibee* told by the pilgrim Chaucer. In this story, a man's daughter is raped and his wife beaten. The rest of the narrative, told in prose sentences that Chaucer translated from Latin and French sources, largely consists of the man's wife, Prudence, lecturing her husband on understanding and forgiveness. Very little happens. The characters are transparent personifications. Its conversations seem to go on in a world divorced from social reality.[12]

Nonetheless, the *Tale of Melibee* was clearly one of the most popular and widely read of the *Canterbury Tales* in the century or so after Chaucer's death in 1400. More manuscript copies of this tale survive than of any other single tale. Those manuscripts are festooned with marginal annotations, ticks, and little hands or scribbles noting valuable sayings. Clearly, this was one of the most important of the doctrinal *Tales* of the whole collection. By contrast, *The Miller's Tale* was never copied separately from the Canterbury collection (a good marker of audience popularity in the decades before print). Other tales were copied separately (*The Clerk's*, *The Prioress's*), but not the Miller's. And yet, for our modern sensibility, the most "Chaucerian" of Chaucer's works is the Miller's: fast-paced, colloquial, sexually charged, and told by a fully realized character.

The differences between these two sets of responses to two very different pieces of the same literary work do not hinge simply on matters of taste. They hinge on changing notions of what literature itself may be and what its social function is. That Chaucer could incorporate both kinds of stories—and a world of others—in his *Canterbury Tales* testifies to his breadth and brilliance. That certain readers liked to copy out one tale and not another does not mean they did not understand or value the other. What it does mean is that one tale was uniquely appropriate for a literate, scholarly, pedagogical world, and that another one was not. It does not mean that *Melibee* is more "medieval" than the *Miller's Tale*. It means that certain people who had access to and skill in writing valued *Melibee* and that the evidence of their work survives.

What it also means is that, at certain times, *The Canterbury Tales* questions its own controlling premise. There are times when it feels more written than spoken. There are times when we must suspend our belief in the fiction of the pilgrims, mounted and moving, actually listening to something. Homer and Virgil may, to the modern reader, illustrate historical differences between oral and literate modes of literature. *The Canterbury Tales*, for its own historical time, represents in itself the ongoing differences between face-to-face performance and reading a text.

Chaucer's description of his work is accurate: it has everything in it, things great and small and moral and holy and dirty and funny. He may invite us to pick and choose but such an invitation is a ruse. For if an author is a good one, he or she does not invite: he or she compels. Our freedom may be limited. Look at Aeneas. His eye roams over Carthage's illustrated walls, much as a reader's eye would scan across a page. He sees the warriors circling Pergamus; elsewhere, he sees the death of Troilus; and elsewhere, still, he sees Achilles despoil Hector's body. He weeps, he mourns. And yet, he cannot take his eyes off of these scenes: he watches in wonder, his stare transfixed, hanging almost helpless before these images.

This is what every author wants: to hold an audience transfixed. To ask us to turn the page is disingenuous. Yes, we may find the *Tale of Melibee* too long, too allegorical, and too opaque for our sensibilities. We may want to turn its leaves and get to something more familiar, more direct, more entertaining (the eternally delightful *Nun's Priest's Tale*, for example, with its amorous talking chickens). But, in the fiction of the *Canterbury Tales*, no one complains—at least not here. Indeed, Chaucer's Host glowingly commends the *Tale of Melibee*. No matter. That is Chaucer's fiction: in an age of reading, the immediacy of lived audience response is an illusion. What matters more for Chaucer's pilgrims, as for Dr. Spock's young children, is the lesson of how to get along in the world. Whether a tale is good or bad, long or short, you have to listen. Some may interrupt (the Franklin breaks into the Squire, the Host stops Chaucer's *Tale of Sir Thopas*, the Knight stanches the Monk), but every interruption in *The Canterbury Tales* ultimately resolves itself, and the poem ends with all its pilgrims willingly an audience for the Parson's concluding sermon.

II.

One lesson in school is how to get along in the world. One lesson in literature is how to get along as an audience. Demodocus may be a great singer. But Odysseus is a great listener, and he has the tact to hide his weeping face. Virgil may be a great teacher, but it takes Dante to imagine himself as his prize student. What *The Canterbury Tales* dramatizes throughout its narrative is the difference between a good and a bad audience. At the heart of Chaucer's poem is the problem of attention, the problem of finishing what one starts out to say, of keeping the interest, the docility, and the benevolence of the audience. What happens if they are inattentive, boisterous, or malign? *The Canterbury Tales* dramatizes a variety of answers to that question, and in the end, it offers up a model for future literary history. Acts of writing after someone become what Chaucer called "quitting." The Knight tells a story of aristocratic lovers. The Miller "quits" that story by turning it into a domestic sex game. The Reeve "quits" the Miller by retelling it as farce with regional dialect. Their section of the *Tales*, or other sections in which characters respond explicitly to previous taletellers, offers up a version of how literary texts are transformed by later writers. Acts of quitting become ways of recasting inherited material to meet new social contexts or aesthetic expectations. Thus, later writers may "quit" earlier ones. Chaucer recasts material from Boccaccio. Spenser will recast material from Chaucer. Milton will recast material from Spenser. Shakespeare rewrites Roman comedy or European tragedy. Source material becomes a quittable subject. Literary history becomes a sequence of rewritings and revisions. A good audience, then, is not simply one that listens. It is one that does so carefully, that attends to the challenges of your story, and that (if it is made up of really good listeners and readers) will retell your tale in its own and creative way.

A literary tradition teaches that the purpose of its study is to bring individuals into communities of feeling, conversation, and understanding. Homer and Virgil, Dante and Chaucer, Shakespeare and Milton, Dickens and Orwell, Bradstreet and Frost and Williams and

Dickinson—all speak and write *to* someone. Within their works, they dramatize scenes of performance and reception. In the process, they show how literature creates a community. Demodocus could not live as singer or performer without the occasion of group feasting. He may be gifted by the Muses, but he lives for the people (his very name, in Greek, means "received by the people").[13] Aeneas needs his courtly audience in Carthage for his story, much as his father, Anchises, will need Aeneas himself as student for his teaching. And after picking fruit, whether welcomed or forbidden, Frost and Williams must verbally reflect on their actions. This is just to say, I am overtired, I am sorry. At the heart of Orwell's *1984* was the drama of aesthetic evaluation. But such a drama must go on before someone else. Winston Smith wants to read with Julia. He imagines the proles rising up, not simply in political resistance, but in something of a shared poetic life, a whole city singing "Oranges and lemons say the bells of St. Clement's."

The social function of the literary tradition is to create an audience of meaningful communication and creative exchange. The goal of Chaucer's Franklin, for example, is less to teach a particular moral lesson than to get his listeners thinking and talking about his complex, enigmatic tale. Which of its many characters, he asks them, was the most "free"—that is, the most generous and understanding to the others? Works of literature have many meanings because they have many readers. The purpose of an audience is to adjudicate among them. Odysseus may be the only one crying at Demodocus's performance. But the fact remains that Alcinous asks him *why* he is crying, and with that question, a new literary performance and a new sense of audience response begins. "Tell me why."

Literature teaches us that all acts of reading are acts of criticism, and all acts of criticism are—at least potentially—autobiographical. We read through our experiences, and the act of reading is inseparably bound up with the moment or condition of that act. Pick up a book and you may remember a rainy afternoon, an airplane journey, or the girl who sat beside you in a college seminar. Such memories are inextricably linked to our experience and understanding of a book. In our retelling of its story or our interpretation of its lines, we may invariably call to mind the contexts in which we experienced it.

The recent turn in literary scholarship towards "book history" has stressed that the physical medium of literary transmission—print, hardback, paperback, digital screen—may bear as much meaning as the author's words. The historical study of what was done to books can tell us as much about literature as the study of what was done with them. Thus, looking at the marginalia of readers, or excerpting texts in commonplace-books, or even the mutilation and defacement of pages and bindings can all tell us something of the sociology of literacy.[14]

I believe that, in addition to such a study, we need to incorporate the personal histories of readers into the ways we make meaning out of texts. To say that every act of criticism is autobiographical does not mean, simply, that we read a book for what we think or feel. It means that every time we write or talk about a book we are recalling a particular moment in our lives, and our narrative of that encounter is precisely that: a story of our reading. As the Dickinson scholar Suzanne Juhasz put it, in a sensitive assessment of her own career, "I remember taking my little volume of her selected poems with me on a camping, trip, placing it close to my sleeping bag...I had not counted on the rock under my back, which is also part of that memory."[15]

I'd like to tell you that I wept when I read Homer, that I shuddered over Orwell, that I laughed at Mr. Dick, or that like Dickinson herself, I felt "the top of my head" come off over her poetry. But what I'll probably remember also is the rock under my back. Our search for meaning remains elusive. We all desire an unmediated felt response. But we must recognize that such responses may be thwarted. We want Odysseus's tears, but sometimes we can't have them. We want to have a felt, immediate response to literature, but sometimes we are too enmeshed in history and irony, in representation and reflection, to have it.

III.

I began this book with a nod to Hayden White, and to his plea for academic literary study as a necessary form of historicizing and ironizing. "The academic scholar cannot," White affirmed, "trade on his or her 'feelings' as a substitute for analysis of a text." The criticism of the classroom does not hinge on reverence but on recollection: not on simply voicing admiration for a writer but distinguishing the social and historical environments that shaped the writer and, in turn, our own reflections on the methods through which we productively disturb the literary text. White pleads for distance rather than immediacy, for deferring the resolutions of analysis. The challenge of the academic study of literature is the challenge of delay. It demands not only an immediacy of response, but also a progressive deferring of interpretation.

Nonetheless, White's is a statement of personal feeling, voiced (or, more accurately, typed) in response to irritation at an online argument offered in social media. My quotation came not from a university press published book or from a widely cited article but from his Facebook post in March 2015. It came to me as one post in a series of exchanges, each precisely timed and dated. It popped up on my screen, not just a statement but an invitation to respond as well. Do I hit "Like"? Do I "Reply?"

Facebook and its attendant forms of social media enable the illusion of immediacy. They create conversations or classrooms, removed from the face-to-face of lived performance. But they fulfill a need. For in the process of reading, liking, and responding, we not only engage with others. We create ourselves. Our Facebook "portraits" become simulacra of the self, created characters that live, much like the figures of a novel, on the screen. Social media thus makes us more than readers. It makes every one of us an author. It enables us to shape a character, to invite others to look on the pictures of the past, to like or laugh or weep.[16]

The Princeton English professor Jeff Nunokawa, in the year I write this, has published a collection of Facebook posts.[17] He claims, in his *Note Book*, that his work grew from a "desire for a feeling of connection." Each entry offers, as its kernel, a quotation from a work of a literature or history. Each posting meditates on chosen texts. In the course of reading the book, we come away with Nunokawa's private canon, his sense of literary history as a provocation to his personal response.

It is one thing to read these postings day-to-day. It is another to read (or re-read) them, bound between hard covers. On Facebook, we may like and comment. We may respond in a manner that creates a virtual classroom or coffee house. The value of the process lies in the group aggregation of reaction. In the book, however, we can only watch. We sit by, turn the pages, and observe the English professor display his wide reading and his sensitivity.

This all may be presented as something new, but I am not sure this is any different from the past. David Copperfield's remembrance of his afternoons in his father's library, "reading as if for life," has, as I have already noted, long been taken as a maxim for the bookish child or the nostalgic academic. We all, in some sense, wish to remember that moment when we found ourselves in books. "People," to recall the words of Martha Nussbaum on this passage, "care for the books they read; and they are changed by what they care for." But this is not a story about people. David Copperfield is not Charles Dickens, and his statement comes not in a memoir but a novel. What we read are the remembered experiences of a fictional character. "David Copperfield" is, from the start, a fictional creation in a double sense: first, by the historical Dickens but second, by the character himself, telling his story as if it were a novel.

David's remembrance, much like our constructions on the webs of social media, go on in the world of "as if." He shows us what Nunokawa shows us: that reading is, in itself, a performance. David's reminiscence invites us to watch him read. It makes him the object of our vision, asking us to measure his past self against its new representations. It transforms a moment of remembered isolation and absorption into a carefully staged act before an audience. Even for David himself, it is an artistically recreated moment: "When I think of it, the picture always rises in my mind." It is as if we look at the character looking at himself, as if he is performing both for himself and for us. And at the close of this reminiscence he explicitly invites us in:

> The reader now understands, as well as I do, what I was when
> I came to that point of my youthful history to which I am now
> coming again.

There are so many layers here, so many things between the original experience of David's joy and our reading of it, that we must work to feel it with him. We are reading him remember himself reading. In the narrative of the moment, we must understand.

At moments such as this one (brilliantly prepared and carefully crafted by Dickens, but comparable to many moments in literary fiction) we understand that all reading is a performance. To engage with the literary tradition is to enact something before others and ourselves. We may read silently, we may be deeply absorbed in a text. We read in bed, we read in rooms. Most of us read alone. But what a person truly devoted to reading will do, what a person passionately loving of and living in a book will do, is read in public. And I think literature teaches us precisely how to do that.

Look at the students in the café or the library. Look at commuters on the subway. Look at the man waiting for a bus, the woman on a city bench. What does it mean to read in public? It means to perform an act of self-absorption before others. It means to be inside yourself while outside. It means (sometimes inadvertently, sometimes deliberately) to make yourself the object of another reader: the person who looks at you trying to understand where you are in your book, in your life. What picture arises in your mind?

We may be reading, now, on phones or iPads, Nooks, and Kindles. But when we take these things out of our rooms, we make ourselves objects of public view. Even at our most private of moments, we are seen. Odysseus knew this, trying in vain to hide his tears from his host. But as soon as Alcinous attends to him, as soon as he sees Odysseus cry, all eyes and ears turn from the singer to the hero. They make him the new Demodocus, as he tells his story for an audience of listeners.

How often have we sat on a plane or café table and turned to an unknown neighbor, rapt in reading, smiling to herself, or wiping off a tear, and asked: What are you reading? This, in the end, is the question that literature wants us to ask. The literary tradition, I have argued here, has both a past and present. Today makes yesterday mean, not only because we interpret history through our own experience, but because the question, "What are you reading?" remains a question asked today about what we began before and continue to do now.

And if we answer it right, we shall give not just the title of the book but the story of our lives. We shall look our neighbor in the eye, we shall try to get along in the world, and as we talk about our books, we shall know that what makes us truly human in this unpoetic world is our continuing appreciation of the pastness of the past, our taste for a tradition made our own, and our need, when we have been inexact in taste, to ask forgiveness.

Notes

1. All quotations for the *Odyssey* are from the Loeb Classical Library text, Homer, *The Odyssey*, ed. and trans. A. T. Murray (Cambridge, Mass.: Harvard University Press, 1919), English translation revised by Timothy Power and Gregory Nagy, text online at <http://www.perseus.tufts.edu/hopper/text?doc=Perseus%3Atext%3A1999.01.0218% 3Abook%3D1>. Cited by book and line number.

2. For the basic, scholarly commentary, see Alfred Heubeck, Stephanie West, and J. B. Hainsworth, *A Commentary on Homer's Odyssey, Volume I Introduction and Books I–VIII* (Oxford: Clarendon Press, 1988); on Book VIII, see 346–85. On the broader questions of the hero as his own poet, and the complex relationships of song and heroism in the Odyssey, see Gregory Nagy, *The Best of the Achaeans: Concepts of the Hero in Archaic Greek Poetry*, rev. ed., (Baltimore: Johns Hopkins University Press, 1999); Pietro Pucci, *Odysseus Polutropos: Intertextual Readings in the Odyssey and the Iliad* (Ithaca: Cornell University Press, 1987); Charles Segal, *Singers, Heroes, and Gods in the Odyssey* (Ithaca: Cornell University Press, 1994); Jenny Strauss Clay, *The Wrath of Athena: Gods and Men in the Odyssey* (London: Rowman & Littlefield, 1996).

3. Quotations from the *Aeneid* are from the English translation of Allen Mandelbaum, *The Aeneid of Virgil* (New York: Bantam Books, 1972). Latin citations are from *Virgil: Eclogues. Georgics. Aeneid: Books 1–6*, ed. G. P. Goold (Cambridge, Mass.: Harvard University Press, 1999). Key guides to criticism and interpretation include Kenneth Quinn, *Virgil's Aeneid: A Critical Description* (Ann Arbor: University of Michigan Press, 1968); Charles Segal, "Art and the Hero: Participation, Detachment, and Narrative Point of View in the *Aeneid*," *Arethusa* 14 (1981): 67–83; Gian Biagio Conte, *The Poetry of Pathos: Studies in Virgilian Epic*, ed., S. J. Harrison (Berkeley and Los Angeles: University of California Press, 2007).

4. See Domenico Comparetti, *Virgil in the Middle Ages*, ed. with a New Introduction by Jan Ziolkowski (Princeton: Princeton University Press, 1997); Christopher Baswell, *Virgil in Medieval England: Figuring the Aeneid from the Twelfth Century to Chaucer* (Cambridge: Cambridge University Press, 1995); Leslie George Whitbread, *Fulgentius the Mythographer* (Columbus: Ohio State University Press, 1971); Bernardis Silvestris, *The Commentary on the First Six Books of Virgil's Aeneid*, trans. Earl G. Schreiber and Thomas E. Maresca (Lincoln: University of Nebraska Press, 1979); Michael Murrin, *The Allegorical Epic* (Chicago: University of Chicago Press, 1980); David Scott Wilson-Okamura, *Virgil in the Renaissance* (Cambridge: Cambridge University Press, 2010).

5. See Friedrich August Wolf, *Prolegomena to Homer, 1795*, trans. Anthony Grafton et al. (Princeton: Princeton University Press, 1985), and the broad overview in James Turner, *Philology: The Forgotten Origins of the Modern Humanities* (Princeton: Princeton University Press, 2014).

6. The one possible representation of writing in Homer is the passage in Book 6 of the *Iliad*, describing the fateful or dangerous symbols (*semata lugra*) inscribed in a folding

tablet that Bellerophontes takes with him to Lykia (168–70). See the discussion in Charles Segal, "Greek Tragedy: Writing, Truth, and the Representation of the Self," in *Interpreting Greek Tragedy: Myth, Poetry, Text* (Ithaca: Cornell University Press, 1986), 75–109.

7. Benjamin Spock, *Baby and Child Care*, 15th edition (New York: Bantam, 1985), 479.

8. Harald Weinrich, *Lethe: Kunst und Kritik des Vergessens* (Munich: C. H. Beck, 1997), trans. Steven Rendall, *Lethe: The Art and Critique of Forgetting* (Ithaca: Cornell University Press, 2004), 136.

9. For the notions of an oral and formulaic poetics behind Homer, see Albert Bates Lord, *The Singer of Tales* (Cambridge, Mass.: Harvard University Press, 1960). For the cultural shifts between oral and literate cultures, Eric Havelock, *The Literate Revolution in Greece and its Cultural Consequences* (Princeton: Princeton University Press, 1982); William V. Harris, *Ancient Literacy* (Cambridge, Mass.: Harvard University Press, 1989); Seth Lerer, *Literacy and Power in Anglo-Saxon Literature* (Lincoln: University of Nebraska Press, 1991); Walter J. Ong, *Orality and Literacy* (London: Routledge, 1982; rev. ed. 2002).

10. For approaches to orality and literacy in Chaucer, the cultures of performance in the late-fourteenth-century English courts, and Chaucer's dramas of reading and interpretation, see the following: Seth Lerer, *Chaucer and His Readers* (Princeton: Princeton University Press, 1993); John Ganim, *Chaucerian Theatricality* (Princeton: Princeton University Press, 1990); Nancy Mason Bradbury, *Writing Aloud: Storytelling in Late Medieval England* (Urbana: University of Illinois Press, 1998); and the essays throughout Lerer, ed., *The Yale Companion to Chaucer* (New Haven: Yale University Press, 2006).

11. The text is from Larry D. Benson, general editor, *The Riverside Chaucer*, 3rd edition (Boston: Houghton Mifflin, 1987); translation mine.

12. For the critical challenges of the *Tale of Melibee*, see David Wallace, *Chaucerian Polity* (Stanford: Stanford University Press, 1997), 212–46.

13. See Carol Dougherty, *The Raft of Odysseus: The Ethnographic Imagination of Homer's Odyssey* (Oxford: Oxford University Press, 2001), 196 n. 39.

14. See the essays collected in Seth Lerer and Leah Price, eds, "The History of the Book and the Idea of Literature," *PMLA* 121 (January 2006); Price, *How to Do Things with Books in Victorian England* (Princeton: Princeton University Press, 2012).

15. "A Life with Emily Dickinson: Surprise and Memory," *Emily Dickinson Journal*, 21 (2012): 80–1.

16. For an eloquent meditation on the challenges of digital literacy and social media to traditions of reading and personal growth, see Andrew Piper, *Book There Was* (Chicago: University of Chicago Press, 2014).

17. Jeff Nunokawa, *Note Book* (Princeton: Princeton University Press, 2015).

Acknowledgments

I am most grateful to Philip Davis and Jacqueline Baker for inviting me to contribute this volume to the Literary Agenda, and for their responses, support, and encouragement throughout my work on the book. Philip provided wonderful guidance, and offered detailed comments on a penultimate draft that have made this a better book. Timothy Hampton read an early draft and provided enlightening responses. Renee Fox brought her expertise as a Victorianist to the first chapters. Deanne Williams read everything as I was writing, and she remains my most treasured interlocutor. Most of this book was drafted during my term as a Keeley Visiting Fellow at Wadham College, Oxford. I am grateful to my colleagues at Wadham, especially Jane Griffiths and Ankhi Mukherjee, for stimulating conversations and a warm welcome. The Bodleian Library, the Wadham College Library, and the English Faculty Library at Oxford were the perfect places to read and write. I am grateful, too, to the University of California at San Diego for providing me research leave to complete this book, and for an Academic Senate grant to facilitate my time at Oxford.

Acknowledgements

Short Bibliography

Erich Auerbach, *Mimesis: The Representation of Reality in Western Literature*, trans. W. R. Trask (Princeton: Princeton University Press, 1957).

Judith Butler, *Gender Trouble* (New York: Routledge, 1990).

T. S. Eliot, *Selected Essays*, 2nd edition (London: Faber & Faber, 1934).

Paul Fussell, *The Great War and Modern Memory* (New York: Oxford University Press, rev. ed., 2000).

Denise Gigante, *Taste: A Literary History* (New Haven: Yale University Press, 2005).

F. R. Leavis, *The Great Tradition: George Eliot, Henry James, Joseph Conrad* (New York: Doubleday, 1954).

Deirdre Shauna Lynch, *Loving Literature: A Cultural History* (Chicago: University of Chicago Press, 2015).

Franco Moretti, *Distant Reading* (London: Verso, 2013).

Ankhi Mukherjee, *What is a Classic? Postcolonial Writing and the Invention of the Canon* (Stanford: Stanford University Press, 2014).

Jeff Nunokawa, *Note Book* (Princeton: Princeton University Press, 2015).

Leah Price, *How to Do Things with Books in Victorian England* (Princeton: Princeton University Press, 2012).

Edward Said, *Beginnings: Intention and Method* (Baltimore: Johns Hopkins University Press, 1975).

Edward Said, *Culture and Imperialism* (New York: Knopf, 1993).

Leo Spitzer, *Representative Essays*, ed. Alban Forcione, Herbert Lindenberger, and Madeline Sutherland (Stanford: Stanford University Press, 1988).

Lionel Trilling, *The Liberal Imagination: Essays on Literature and Society* (New York: New York Review Books, 2008).

Hayden White, *Metahistory: The Historical Imagination in Nineteenth-Century Europe* (Baltimore: Johns Hopkins University Press, 1975).

Index